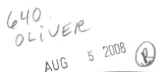

WITHDRAWN

SORTED!

The ultimate guide to organising your life – once and for all

bills to pay

bills paid

entertainment

school stuff

memorabilia

Lissanne Oliver

Hardie Grant Books

Published in 2007
by Hardie Grant Books
85 High Street
Prahran, Victoria 3181, Australia
www.hardiegrant.com.au

Cataloguing-in-Publication data:

   Oliver, Lissanne.
   Sorted!: the ultimate guide to organising your life –
   once and for all.

   ISBN 9 78 1 74066 520 9 (pbk.).

   1. Simplicity. 2. Orderliness. I. Title.

   640

Cover and text design by saso content & design pty ltd
Photography by Joe Ashton
Author photograph by Paul Wesley-Smith, a VISUAL life photography
Propping and styling by Lissanne Oliver
Index by Fay Donlevy
Printed and bound in China by SNP Leefung

Every effort has been made to incorporate up-to-date information
and statistics. The publishers regret any errors and omissions
and invite readers to contribute additional relevant information
to Hardie Grant Books.

10 9 8 7 6 5 4 3 2

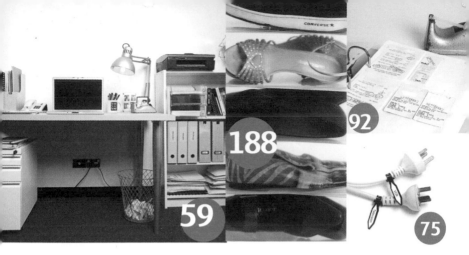

Contents

Introduction

This book is for anyone who's ever:

- been lost in a sea of paper
- had to pay a late-payment fee
- said 'it's here somewhere'
- had trouble closing cupboard doors
- stumbled around in the morning trying to find matching shoes
- lost a cheque, precious photo or special trinket
- felt they didn't know where to start
- purchased something again because they've 'lost' the original
- felt overwhelmed by the thought of organising their stuff
- wanted simple solutions to everyday problems
- wanted to organise their space without spending a fortune
- felt frustrated that boxes and tubs don't fix the problem (without knowing why)
- wanted to learn time- and money-saving ways to complete tasks.

No one teaches us how to be organised, yet it's a fundamental life skill that is crucial to personal and professional success. We all know that a lack of organisation and efficiency is costly, stressful and time-consuming. Being organised is like having a well-serviced life: things aren't 'lost'; paperwork doesn't pile up; time isn't wasted trying to find things; money isn't squandered double-buying items or having to replace lost objects. Finding a place for everything and putting everything in its place also means having more time for the good stuff – time with your partner or family, or time spent just relaxing. The benefits are far-reaching.

You might feel frustrated by your lack of organisation, and you probably find the thought of having to fix things *completely over-whelming*. The process becomes difficult because you don't know how to start or find it hard to make time. When attempts are abandoned, the problem is compounded and causes guilt.

In this book, I will teach you that anyone can become organised; it's a skill that can be learnt. I will share what I have discovered through years of professional organising, consulting in homes and offices, and teaching in workshops around Australia. So turn over a new leaf and learn to live more efficiently and effectively. Get organised! Every small step contributes to a better quality of life.

This book has three parts:

- Getting sorted
- Truths and techniques
- Recipes.

The 'recipes' in the final section of the book are grouped into four main areas:

- Work
- Paper
- On the go
- Living.

In this book, I will help you to:

- understand the fundamental principles of being organised
- learn crucial organising skills
- debunk some common organising myths
- solve focus and time-management problems
- identify the tools required to simplify your busy life and space
- realistically project-manage organising tasks
- declutter significant areas of your home, work space and life
- reduce the volume
- formulate a strategy
- feel confident about getting things under control
- actually have fun in the process.

Happy sorting!

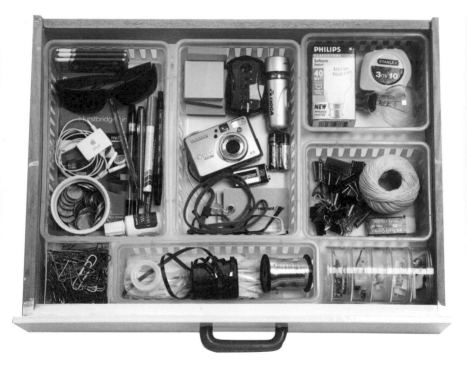

Getting sorted

1

Why get sorted?

Congratulations on taking a positive step towards getting organised. This book is full of tips and information that will potentially change your life. I am passionate about empowering you so that you can take charge and do it yourself. This book is different in that it busts many myths and actually shows you, step by step, *how* to get organised. Learning is doing, so give it a go.

The benefits are life changing – successful people are generally highly organised, or they have highly organised people supporting them. Don't underestimate the value of being on top of things. You will have loads more time (yes!), save buckets of money and avoid lots of frustration. Being efficient will give you more choices about how you spend your time. Being organised will allow you the freedom to explore your passions and dreams.

What's important to you? What do you want your space to be like? Imagine how you would like to spend your time. Daydream. If you don't dream it, it can't be. Foster an approach that includes visualising a beautiful, welcoming, productive space, an efficient and less stressful life, less money wasted. You can 'roll it out'; that is, you can implement your changes one by one, rather than all at once. Change takes time.

It's also important to know what motivates you – we are good at different things for different reasons. Sir Bob Geldof put it this way: 'I do politics for my head, I do business for my pocket, I do music for my soul and I do family for my heart'.

Artist Andy Warhol had the most creative approach to managing his stuff. The website of the Andy Warhol Museum describes his approach:

> The highlight of the archives collection is Warhol's Time Capsules. This serial work, spanning a thirty-year period from the early 1960s to the late 1980s, consists of 610 standard sized cardboard boxes, which Warhol, beginning in 1974, filled, sealed and sent to storage. Warhol used these boxes to manage the bewildering quantity of material that routinely passed through his life. Photographs, newspapers and magazines, fan letters, business and personal correspondence, artwork, source images for artwork, books, exhibition catalogues, and telephone messages, along with objects and countless examples of ephemera, such as announcements for poetry readings and dinner invitations, were placed on an almost daily basis into a box kept conveniently next to his desk.
>
> www.warhol.org/collections/archives.html

What a spectacular method! It's a shame we can't all be famous artists. I saw Warhol's Time Capsules a few years back. The content wasn't as fascinating as I thought it might be, but the concept still grabs me. I love the idea that gathering all that stuff was not only Andy's way of managing his belongings, but it also qualifies as art.

When life runs efficiently, we gain more time and money, which allows us to make better choices. Let's say you want to buy a property but have left organising the finance to the last minute. You might only find one lender able to turn things around in time; if you'd been organised and planned ahead, you could have shopped for the best interest rates, fees and charges. Or say you're on holidays and want to take a tour. If only you'd booked ahead, you would have scored the $50 early-bird discount. Or you might arrive late for a friend's party because you didn't look up the address in the street directory, and you also failed to buy a gift in time. Embarrassing. Costly. Stressful.

How to get sorted

Being organised is about operating efficiently. It's about using time wisely. It's also about retrieval: can you find what you need when you need it? It takes planning and time management. Being organised is not about being anal. Being organised is not about throwing everything out (although less is best since there's less to organise).

You could liken being organised to neat ball of string. You are able to find the end of the string, take what you need and put it away in its rightful place. You can grab it in a hurry and still do the job. (And let's face it: life is often about doing things in a rush because of the demands on our time.) A tangled mess of string is disorganised and inefficient. You look at it and immediately feel overwhelmed. Where to start? It will take time, focus and energy to untangle the string, smooth out the knots and rewind it into some semblance of order.

What's your understanding of being organised and efficient?

_____

_____

_____

Let me differentiate between neat and organised, as people often confuse the two.

- *Neat* can be defined as visual order.
- *Organised* can be defined as efficient order.

In the section called 'Truths and techniques' I will share with you the philosophies and techniques I use in consulting sessions with clients. I am going to teach you how to dramatically change your space and how to easily manage the stuff in your life. It's easy when you know how! Make sure you read this section first and refer back to it whenever you feel stuck or lack clarity.

The final section – 'Recipes' – provides step-by-step instructions and guidance on how to go about organising specific areas of your home, work and life. Before you get started on any recipe, get yourself a drink and put on some music or the radio (but not talkback radio as it's distracting). I promise you: it's more exciting than housework! It's definitely cathartic too. Just take things one step at a time and you will see some amazing results. And remember that things often get worse before they get better. Creating order sometimes involves creating what appears to be more disorder before you can make it right.

Set a goal and be clear and concise about what you want to achieve. Get your life and space in order and tasks will be a joy, not a chore. The simple recipes in this book allow for plenty of choice and flexibility. Manage paper and information, create spacious work and play areas, and feel more in control and less overwhelmed. In a nutshell, you will need to:

- have a plan (that's what the recipes are for)
- clear the mess
- reorder the rest
- maintain your efforts.

Being organised is a life skill. Let me show you how easy it really is. In this book, I will share many simple organising tips and techniques. Now it's up to you. Good luck.

Clutter

The vast majority of us collect, own and store more stuff than we could ever possibly need. The definition of clutter is anything you don't love, don't use and don't need. Loving, needing and using what you have brings clarity and peace of mind, and it facilitates focus. It enables our physical and mental energy to be better used elsewhere.

Decluttering is only a *part* of being organised, but more often than not, it's the first step. You'll need to address the clutter in order to have a positive result. Once you've culled, there is less content to manage and you are only putting effort into organising *what matters*.

Both homes and businesses are susceptible to clutter. The most commonly hoarded items are:

- paper
- digital information
- stationery
- magazines
- clothes
- all forms of electrical equipment, working or not. (A businesswoman I know has a dinosaur of a photocopier even though there are several all-in-one fax-printer-scanners in her office. The old copier chews up an enormous amount of room and is rarely, if ever, turned on. It's the size of a small cubby house and was sucking the energy out of that office. It dragged me down just looking at it.)

I am a former hoarder. I once moved house with piles of magazines and unread newspapers. I was barely out of my teens. A few years later, a removalist asked me why I had three sewing machines. Embarrassed, I mumbled that only one of them worked. Right through my twenties, I shopped furiously at garage sales, op shops and fetes, bringing home boxes and bags full of cheap, interesting stuff, much of it retro collectables, but some of it never quite right. I became an expert garage saler and recycler in order to create more space. (Best garage sale tip: you make your money on the $1 and $2 items; it all adds up.) I have torn things out of magazines, collected catalogues, bookmarked endless websites, taken too many digital photos and saved the ticket from practically every concert I've ever been to. As a young girl, I even saved every bus ticket. Why, I don't exactly know.

Being a hoarder is about making poor choices – choices that we need to be mindful of every day, much like the choices we make about what to put into our bodies. Keeping the balance is important. It deserves your attention because the cost is high. Avoid clutter and you will save time, money and energy in your day-to-day life. If you have too much clutter, make 'if in doubt, chuck it out' your mantra. Get rid of the dead wood; complete or delete projects; move on from the past and keep *only* what counts.

Have a permanent 'go' box – a box to go to charity that lives near the front door. Items are added to it as you see or touch them: trousers that no longer fit, unwanted Tupperware, excess stationery. Even at my house, this box is fed on a regular basis. It feels so good to let go of things that are excess to my needs. This week I added two old cushion covers, a dress that is too big, a top that doesn't fit and some old notepaper I like but will never use. As soon as it's full, I kiss it goodbye and take it to the local op shop. And I've never missed a single item. In fact, I can barely recall the items I've let go.

You can't have everything. Where would you put it all? It's about what you will get to keep, not about what you will lose.

● Mythbuster: storage

There's a whole industry based around storing your stuff: off-site storage; shops that sell nothing but containers; products that promise to organise your life; magazines that promote pretty coloured boxes. While these products and services definitely have their place (particularly when used correctly), they generally don't fix the problem. Being organised does not mean purchasing a dozen 80-litre plastic tubs and sticking everything in them. It's a common technique and is well intended. I understand the temptation. But I'm here to tell you: containers won't fix your stuff.

Many clients have told me that they wasted a lot of money on 'organising products' simply because they were desperate for a solution. When I've finished a session with a client, it's not uncommon to end up with a pile of unneeded products and containers.

My belief is that you must deal with the content. Containers and off-site storage won't fix the problem; indeed, they often compound it, as journalist Deidre Macken observed:

> … more Australians now belong to the storage set. The storers prefer to stow than throw because the stuff costs – so much or because they can't face up to the mistake – 120 litres of mistakes or 5 cubic metres of mistakes - or because they fear the future may be less bountiful.
>
> For them, the act of moving stuff from a regular storage vessel, say a wardrobe, into a clear plastic tub is a virtuous act. They're the ones who frequent Officeworks for clear plastic tray stacks, vacuum-seal packs and blister wrap when they 'clean out' the office. They're the ones who used to have sheds but now have a second home.

Australian Financial Review

Off-site storage does have its place, however, and is best used in instances like these:

- You run a business from home and that business involves shipping products or sending information packs. Your home doesn't have the space you need for your stock, so off-site storage provides you with a tax-deductible solution.
- You're a musician and have lots of expensive equipment that you take to and from gigs. Your house isn't necessarily that secure, so off-site storage enables you to store your gear without worry. Off-site storage also offers you the convenience of bumping in and out at all hours without disturbing the neighbours.
- You are moving interstate for a 12-month contract at work, so after culling (important!), you store your goods and chattels for a time to see if you will make a more permanent move.
- You're renovating and need a *temporary* home for your belongings.
- You live in an itsy-bitsy, teeny-weeny studio apartment, so all your ski gear, out-of-season clothes, have-to-have memorabilia and old tax returns live off site.

Specialist products and containers are best used in situations such as these:

- You've had a session with a Professional Organiser, who has made specific product recommendations to you.
- You've seen a particular product used by a friend or colleague with great success (and you have exactly the same problem to fix).
- You have already culled but would like to store baby clothes, Christmas decorations and/or old tax documentation.

Being organised

Organised people are not rocket scientists, nor are they necessarily high achievers. Some organised folk are anal (we all know one or two). But mostly they are just a little bit more tuned in, and they are better at getting on with things – even things they don't like doing. Organised people pay attention. They are often paying attention because they are more focused than most. They are mindful of balance. They take time to get organised. They are generally planners.

If you're not organised, you may be a slave to playing 'catch up'. Unorganised people are typically overwhelmed with paper, a backlog of emails, missed appointments and significant dates, late fees for DVDs and library books, unfinished projects, and a shed or spare room full of stuff that they're 'going to get to later'. There's the frustration of losing a valuable telephone number or a missed business opportunity because you couldn't manage to get the pitch in on time. And this leads to a reputation for running late, a reputation for being unreliable. All these things – and more – make for a stressful, costly existence.

Why aren't you organised? It could be for a number of reasons:

- You've never been taught.
- Your upbringing was strict and structured and super neat, and you have reacted to that.
- Your upbringing was relaxed and casual, unstructured and untidy.
- You're creative.
- You've experienced change (a house or office move; more demands on your time as a result of having children; a new role at work; a relationship breakdown; an illness or a major event like the death of someone close to you).
- You feel you don't have the skills.
- You feel guilty about the situation and have chosen to ignore it.
- You feel you are too busy and/or being organised is a low priority.

It doesn't matter what your reasons are: the solutions are all the same. The main criteria for successful and permanent change are:

- making a long-term commitment
- prioritising what needs to be done
- rewarding yourself for goals achieved (no matter how small)
- understanding that being organised is an ongoing process
- keeping a balance.

Procrastination

Put simply, procrastination is a bad habit. Habits can be changed, and research shows this can happen in as little as a couple of weeks if you are consistent with your efforts. Procrastination is also a fine art. Lots of us (including me) are highly skilled practitioners. I could procrastinate for Australia. Then there's the internet – humankind's greatest invention for procrastination (along with television, which I've heard referred to as 'that great time-wasting machine').

On occasions, procrastination can be immensely useful. Creative people, for instance, often need to dip in and out of projects. Or you may need some quiet time to fully digest a report or complete a complex document or project. But the real trick is knowing *when* it's appropriate to procrastinate. It's about being selective and making better choices. Shuffling deck chairs on the *Titanic* is not in your best interests. So while procrastination has its good side, more often than not it's a destructive habit. It serves only to make us feel bad about ourselves, to delay the inevitable, to put us behind the eight ball. It generally complicates the outcome, impedes success and compromises brilliance.

Procrastination is generally born of fear, and fear is an extremely powerful demotivator:

- I'm frightened I won't do a good job.
- I'm frightened I'll be judged on the end result of that job (a very common fear among students and perfectionists, the rationale being that if the work is never complete, it can never be fully judged).
- I'm fearful the job is too big.
- I'm fearful of the unknown.
- I'm just fearful.

There are a great many reasons for procrastination, but my advice is simple: get on with it or get over it.

- If the job is big, simply break it down into smaller chunks.
- If the fear is about performance, understand that you cannot know unless you actually *try*.
- Change is scary. But the unknown is never as scary as you might imagine. Fear can be powerful in this context, so understand that a positive attitude and your willingness to try are what's most important.

Limbo land is unproductive and disheartening. Be empowered. Make the choice to get on with it. Moving forward with a task, no matter how unpleasant, is a very 'feel good' thing to do. Walk to your desk and say, 'I'm going to make the two phone calls I most want to avoid'. Then do it. The sense of relief and pride will be a sensational reward.

Choices

We're often overwhelmed with choice. Making the 'right' decision can be a complex procedure. Be aware of the choices that are offered, and try to focus on what really matters. I heard once that humans operate best with seven choices or less, and I think this is true. Present twenty-four kinds of paper, and decision making becomes difficult. Present three choices, and life suddenly gets a whole lot easier. Latte, cappuccino, flat white, long black, macchiato, fluffy chino, short black, iced coffee? No wonder I always order surprise coffee! I find such decisions trivial. I'd rather spend my mental energy on the bigger picture.

Decision fatigue can hit when we are presented with too many choices or when too many decisions need to be made (like when you're moving house or office). The best thing to do is to take a break. I recently went car shopping. I test drove the first vehicle, and before I'd pulled away from the car park, I phoned my cousin Andrew, who knows cars, for a bit of advice. Was it OK to buy the first car I drove? It almost seemed too simple. But I felt obliged to soldier on. Four cars later, I purchased one. It was pretty much the same as the first one. There's no doubt the decision seemed protracted; every car had all the features I wanted and needed.

Choice *is* important for the bigger decisions: housing, health care, education, food, money, voting, relationships, spiritual beliefs and so on. My advice is not to agonise over the small stuff.

Detail

If you are detail oriented, you have your work cut out for you. Being a slave to the minutiae is a dangerous thing. It will suck your time and energy and contribute to your lack of organisation in a very big way. Don't you have better things to do with your time? You might even be what I call an 'information junkie'. For you, too much information is not enough. My suggestion to you is to set boundaries: you will never be able to swim that whole ocean, so learn to ride the wave better.

Try not to get lost in the finer details: paper, photos, jewellery, memorabilia, flotsam and jetsam – basically, anything small and time-consuming. I call the organisation of these things 'fine tuning', and it can be done at a later date. Focus on bigger items; for example, significant pieces of furniture; storage; bookcases and cabinets; shoes; bedding; hanging clothes; sporting goods; and luggage. Systematically work your way from the largest items to the smallest. Tasks like untangling jewellery, looking at business cards and sorting through pens and pencils are best done while watching television or as a bit of a break.

The detail in everyday life is overwhelming: brochures, phone numbers, text messages, digital photos, junk mail, email, passwords,

ATM slips, login details, browser bookmarks, filenames, receipt numbers (I recently received a 19-digit receipt number for paying one bill over the phone), version control, interest rates, virus protection, currency conversion, bank statements, receipts, flight numbers, ABN numbers, post office box numbers, postcodes, BPAY, client numbers, catalogues, automated phone menus, discount coupons, client numbers, registration numbers, newspapers, pop-up advertising, pull-down menus,

kids' artwork, school newsletters. No wonder we're all tired and cranky.

There's a lot of detail competing for our attention. This ocean of detail is overwhelming and sometimes confusing. Stick to the things you absolutely have to know (and keep reasonable records if necessary), but let go of the detail that doesn't matter. Paying attention to detail is worthwhile when spelling someone's name, filling out forms or perusing legal contracts. But it's OK to ignore some detail. It's good to have balance and to keep an eye on the bigger stuff.

Want versus need

The stuff in our space can overwhelm us because we're in 'want' mode all the time. I want it because everyone else has one, because I got this nice shopping bag with it, because it's how I blow off stress, because I have a credit card, because it's on sale. That's all fine, and I'm not anti-consumerism (OK, well, maybe a little), but I think we should be wiser with our purchasing. Avoid the 'wants'. We should buy better quality stuff that we really love or genuinely need. If you love your discount or two-dollar shops, you probably think you're getting a bargain. But it's not usually so: cheap and nasty purchases don't last, don't perform well and aren't well designed in terms of function and form. It's often about buying it simply because it's cheap.

Our grandparents, or even our parents, bought only what they needed when they first married. They would have saved to purchase a dining table, a lounge suite, a bed and dresser, a decent set of pots and pans. There was no credit card or six months interest free, no fast-food mentality. They might have even done without while they saved up. They would have bought the best quality they could afford because they knew it would have to last a lifetime. Apply this philosophy to your purchases. Aim to own it for a long time, if not a lifetime. Make sure whatever furniture you own is *versatile* and has more than one use: a dining table that could also be a desk, a couch that becomes a sofa bed, freestanding shelving that could be adapted to any room. A good example is a simple cube or crate. It's a container in its own right (for sporting gear); turned on its side, it becomes a shelf with two flat surfaces (which could be wall mounted), or upturned it can become a seat or step. Configured with other cubes, you have instant, trans-portable storage that offers the ultimate in flexibility.

Invest in good 'dailies'. A daily is anything used daily: lipstick, coathangers, tea, shoes, underwear, bed, crockery, cutlery, pens and so on. Invest in good-quality items and use the 'good stuff' in your life.

- *Want* means buying a new suitcase because you like the look of it or because a friend buys one.
- *Need* means replacing that suitcase because the tear can't be repaired in a way that maintains the integrity of the bag. Or your needs might have changed and you genuinely require a different size.

Falling into the cheap trap is dangerous. Let's say you see something cheap – a pair of shoes, for example. They're on sale. You buy them *because they're cheap*. But would you have bought them if they had been full retail price? Or are you buying them because you think you've got a bargain? I once bought three pairs of Doctor Marten's sample shoes. They were $50 each, which is a massive discount from the $120+ price tag they normally carry. One pair hurt like hell (out). One pair I loved but the colour wasn't me (eventually they went out too). The third pair is much loved and I am still wearing them five years later (in). My lesson was that one pair really cost me the price of three pairs. I paid the equivalent of a brand new, full-retail-price pair of Docs. So I didn't save anything at all. It just cost me time and hassle to find new homes for the extra two pairs (the bin and a garage sale). So the favoured pair really weren't that cheap.

Using cheap potting mix will mean your valued indoor plants will never look their best – some of the generic brands are nothing more than sawdust. Investing in the best quality you can afford – ideally, a mix suitable for pots – will see your house plants flourish and prosper.

Be mindful of sales. Go hard, but shop only for what you will use, absolutely love or desperately need. Regardless of the price, if it's not loved, used or needed, it's not a bargain.

Inside a Professional Organiser's tool kit

Getting organised is easy; anyone can do it. You don't need lots of fancy equipment. My Professional Organiser's tool kit shows you everything you need to get the job done.

There are many basic tools that will help you in your journey to becoming organised. When I consult, I take a full tool kit, stocked with many handy tools and supplies. Everyone always wants to know what's in my box of tricks. The majority of my tool-box items are used in the recipes in this book and can easily be sourced at a stationery supplier. A few bits and pieces might also come from the hardware store, super-market, electronics store, or discount or two-dollar shop. While none of these things are particularly expensive, it's good to understand that the right tools and equipment are an investment in your quest to become organised. So buy the best quality you can afford.

- **Lever arch file ($1.50+)**
  The *best kind* is the kind without metal edges – metal will scrape your shelving.
  Great tip: if you don't overload them, they're easier to handle.
- **Packing tape ($3)**
  The *best kind*: as a general rule, the clearer the tape, the better the quality.
  Great tip: don't buy the brown tape, as it leaves an ugly brown sticky residue.

- **Tape measure ($20)**

  The *best kind* is one with a 'lock' to hold in place when opening. Avoid the really cheap generic kind – you get what you pay for. *Great tip:* tape measures come in different lengths and generally start at 3 metres. An 8-metre tape measure should be ample for general use. A tape measure that offers both imperial and metric measures is more versatile.

- **Pens ($1.50+)**

  The *best kind* is any kind you *love* using. My personal preference is for a Staedtler Stick or Bic Cristal medium tip. *Great tip:* avoid clutter by not owning too many pens. Twenty is plenty at your desk. Don't hoard pens.

- **Cable ties ($1.50+)**

  The *best kind*; plastic are great but velcro are reusable. *Great tip:* a mixed pack of sizes should cover just about all uses.

- **Rechargeable batteries ($1.50+)**

  The *best kind* depends on the appliance. Ask when you purchase. *Great tip:* recycle your old batteries.

- **Sticky tape ($4.30)**

  The *best kind* is Scotch tape. It looks nice, feels smooth and sticks beautifully. It's pricey but a small pleasure. *Great tip:* don't let it roll around in a drawer getting dusty. Chuck it out when it's old and crusty.

- **Stapler ($5+)**

  The *best kind* is one that feels nice in your hand and is easy to use –
  ergonomics are important with everyday tools.

  Great tip: buy plenty of staples when you buy your stapler.

- **Blade ($5+)**

  The *best kind* is one with a retractable blade, as it will help prevent
  accidents. I like the NT Cutter or OLFA blade.

  Great tip: get the kind that allows you to snap the end of the blade
  off so you're guaranteed sharp cutting. Add a metal ruler and
  cutting mat for safe, accurate cutting.

- **Sticky notes ($3+)**

  The *best kind* are the 3M Post-It Notes. They are the original and
  best. Generic brands leave a residue on the next sticky note that
  you can't easily write over.

  Great tip: get three sizes – small, medium and large.

- **Blu Tack ($5)**

  The *best kind* is fresh, clean and dust free.

  Great tip: remember to 'roll it off' painted surfaces.

- **Labelmaker tape ($12 each)**

  The *best kind* is the kind that has a split in the backing paper – it's
  really easy to separate.

  Great tip: did you know about iron-on fabric tape? It's great for
  anything washable.

- **Labelmaker ($50+)**

  The *best kind* is the kind with a QWERTY keyboard – just like a
  regular keyboard.

  Great tip: check if yours takes fabric tape.

- **Fasteners ($7)**
  The *best kind* are Esselte Nalclip fasteners; you use a special dispenser, and they slide on and slide off, so they're reusable and don't damage your paper.
  Great tip: different sizes accommodate different thicknesses of document.

- **Texta ($2.24)**
  The *best kind* is a thick chisel tip, which will give you cleaner, more attractive writing. A fine tip is best for labelling CDs and so on.
  Great tip: keep one in your pocket when sorting so it's always on hand.

- **Pencil and eraser ($1.50+)**
  The *best kind* of pencil is an HB because it's dark.
  Great tip: keep your pencils sharp.

- **Display book ($1.50+)**
  The *best kind* are the ones with removable pages – such as Marbig Kwik Zip A4 refillable display books – so you can swap stuff around.
  Great tip: use different coloured folders for different categories of information.

- **Gaffer tape ($15+)**
  The *best kind* is branded gaffer tape, which is better quality. Avoid the really cheap stuff. Gaffer tape is great for all kinds of repairs that glue won't help.
  Great tip: a gaffer (lighting technician) never uses scissors. Follow their lead and don't cut; instead, simply tear sharply across the grain of the webbing – it's like fabric. Gaffer tape is sometimes called 'duct tape'.

- **Map pins ($1.50+)**
  The *best kind* are the ones with the traditional ball shape, which are usually easiest to handle.
  Great tip: keep them right near your pin board (or, better still, *on* your pin board).
- **Dividers ($1.50+)**
  The *best kind* are reinforced plastic and come in a pack of five. They are versatile and sturdy.
  Great tip: paper dividers are fine but not designed for frequent use.
- **Letter files ($3 for a pack of 10)**
  The *best kind* are those with a half-moon finger tab for ease of opening.
  Great tip: use them for segmenting information.
- **File fasteners (from $5 for a pack of 50)**
  The *best kind* are Celco slide clips (metal) or Avery Tubeclip file fasteners (plastic).
  Great tip: File fasteners are excellent for archiving.
- **Sheet protectors ($5 for a pack of 100)**
  The *best kind* are the slightly higher quality pockets with a smoother plastic finish.
  Great tip: use them for segmenting information.
- **Shelf splits ($2.50+)**
  The *best kind*: IKEA make fantastic solid metal shelf splits (VARIERA shelf inserts, available in small and large), but the plastic and metal fold-up kind from the two-dollar shop are also good, provided you don't put too much weight on them.
  Great tip: use them to double your horizontal storage space. They're great in the pantry or within a stationery cupboard.

- **Recycling bin (free from your local council)**
  The *best kind* is the largest kind you can get your hands on.
  Great tip: shred sensitive documents before
  bagging them in a large envelope or paper bag
  and recycling.
- **Magazine holders ($9+)**
  The *best kind* is anything *solid*; go for rigid
  plastic or timber.
  Great tip: don't waste your money on the
  flimsy cardboard ones.

- **Rubber bands ($1.50+)**
  The *best kind* is a small bag of assorted sizes.
  Great tip: rubber bands won't last forever, so if yours are brittle,
  they're ready for the bin.
- **Rubbish bin ($1.50+)**
  The *best kind* is the largest kind you can get your hands on.
  Great tip: empty your bin regularly – *before* it overflows.
- **Bulldog clips (10+ cents)**
  The *best kind* are the fold back kind as they will store completely flat
  and not get in the way.
  Great tip: keeping a range of sizes on hand will help you sort any
  paper bundles out fast.
- **Archive boxes ($3+ each)**
  The *best kind* are any with a hinged lid and double walls.
  Off-site storage and removal companies sell them.
  Great tip: label the box well so you know the contents.

2 Truths and techniques

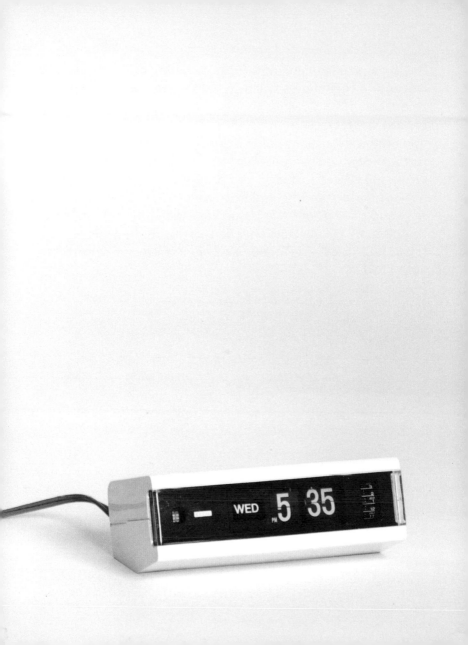

Having a plan is really important. Knowing a few organising truths and techniques will also help make your journey smoother. In some ways, the philosophies and the thinking behind the recipes are more important than the actual implementation. Some of the truths may well move you further forward than you ever thought possible. If you've struggled to get sorted in the past, these ideas are crucial to your understanding and potential success. Take time to read and think about the issues raised and how they apply to your particular situation. The techniques will show you the simplest, most effective and smartest ways to sort your stuff.

Truths: where to start

One of the hardest things is to know where to start. Don't try to tackle everything in one go – you'll quickly feel overwhelmed. Finding – or maintaining – motivation might also be a problem for you. Sometimes just starting will make a difference. The motivation will follow. Pain is also a great motivator. You could wait until the situation gets really bad, really desperate, and then do something about it (but prevention is better than cure).

Here are some more ideas:

- *Start with something easy.*
  You will achieve a good result in a shorter period of time and fast-track your sense of achievement. For instance, you could begin by tackling a small bathroom cupboard, the papers on your desktop, or the top drawer in the hall stand.

An easy area I can start with is

_____

_____

- *Start with an area that currently costs you time or money, or causes you stress.*
  Do you have no system for paying bills, or for filing paperwork?
  Do you constantly lose your keys or precious memorabilia?
  Start by organising just one of these areas and you will immediately

reward yourself with the result. Simply begin by making a list of specific things you want to fix. For example, not getting your tax paperwork in order might be costing you money.

Something that costs me is

_____

_____

- *Start anywhere.*
  If you have a lot to tackle, it really doesn't matter where you start. *Making a start* is the important part.

Something that I've been avoiding is

_____

_____

Truths: making space

Do you have room to move? It's all about boundaries. Our home or office represents one boundary. Each room within that space represents another boundary. Each cupboard, bookshelf and drawer is another boundary again. Our stuff will expand to fill the boundaries – it's human nature. So, if you increase your space – by moving to a larger home, for example – your stuff will simply expand to fit. You will collect more stuff; you will bring more into your space. (Tip: in a small space, the most valuable real estate is the floor. Keep it as clear as possible.)

But space isn't always physical. Having enough head space is also important in order to allow things to flow, to get energy going. Meditating or quiet time is a good example of how we can create more head space. Mentally and physically scale back your boundaries and the stuff that fills them. Set yourself the challenge of visualising what designers call 'white space'. This is the area in a magazine or book that is left empty. It's often a block of colour or a just a blank space without text or images – just like the space below.

White space might be some empty space on your bookshelf, a clear bench or desktop, a made bed. It's a place where your eyes and brain can rest. Acknowledge that everything in your space represents your past and your present. You need to allow yourself room for the future. Empty space doesn't have to be filled.

I would like to make space for

_____

_____

It's not wise or practical to hang on to everything from the past. Things change; what was once important to you may not be important now. Sometimes we develop a relationship with things based on history: the longer you own something, the greater the attachment. This means that something that wasn't originally important becomes important simply because of the length of time you've owned it. That's a dangerous way to think and will probably see you drowning in stuff.

Life is constantly changing, and if you understand that your relationship with your stuff changes, and that your needs and desires change, you will find it a lot easier to let go. Uni notes? They were once of great value. But ten, fifteen or twenty years later, are they still important – really important? No, their purpose has been served, and the best record you can keep of your university years is the single piece of paper that matters: your degree.

Truths: the numbers game

Here's one of the single most powerful tools you can use to organise your space. It's a numbers game. There are two ways to play.

The Pareto rule

I love the Pareto rule. Vilfredo Pareto was a nineteenth-century Italian economist who observed that 80 per cent of Italy's wealth was owned by 20 per cent of the population:

- Twenty per cent of all your actions will account for 80 per cent of your results.
- Twenty per cent of your customers will account for 80 per cent of your sales.
- Twenty per cent of your products and services will account for 80 per cent of the value of what you do.

Another way of putting it is that if you have a list of ten tasks, two of those tasks will be far more valuable than the other eight tasks put together. Each of the tasks may take the same time to accomplish, but one or two of the tasks may contribute five or ten times the value. Sometimes just one task can be worth more than the other nine together. The Pareto rule relates to efficiency. It means focusing on the stuff that matters rather than spreading yourself thin.

I believe this theory applies to far more than just business or economics:

- Twenty per cent of your clothes will be worn 80 per cent of the time (think of your favourite jeans).
- Twenty per cent of the stationery you own will be used 80 per cent of the time; the rest should be let go (think of blank paper and your favourite pen).
- Twenty per cent of the tools and equipment in your kitchen are used 80 per cent of the time (think of your toaster, a good knife and your cutlery).

Percentages

Look at the cupboard, room, drawer or container you need to tackle. Out of the total contents – 100 per cent – what percentage do you need to keep to have a great life? Is it 40 per cent, 50 per cent or 60 per cent? You will probably pick a number in this range. Through many years of consulting, my experience tells me that this is about the mark. However, if you up the ante and aim a little higher, you will be richly rewarded. You won't be bogged down spending time (or thinking about spending time) maintaining stuff you don't really need. Physical stuff can take a lot of your energy – even if you are only looking at it. Having space to rest is very important since our lives are jam-packed with things, events, demands and responsibilities. We're time poor; we've got kids; we run a home office; we work long hours; we don't know whether to move or renovate. We juggle social events, BAS, volunteering, maintaining the family pet's health. We try to get away on holidays, try to keep up studying, try to get enough sleep, try to remember to get the car serviced. A parent falls ill or a partner becomes pregnant, and we fall off the wagon in terms of staying on top of things. It's little wonder!

Keeping life simple and being organised really helps us to manage all our responsibilities and commitments. Less is best; more is a chore.

Some other numbers games you can play:

- one place to keep things
- two favourite colours for pens or stationery
- three boxes for three decades of memorabilia
- twelve decent Tupperware containers
- fifty coathangers, and so on.

If, just once a day, you discard one item that you no longer need, that's 365 items every year.

In considering my belongings overall, I would like to lose _____ per cent to make my life more balanced.

Truths: balance

Balancing the stuff in your life is a skill you can learn. It can be likened to dieting. If you want to lose weight, the solution is not rocket science. Take in fewer calories, watch your portion sizes, and avoid alcohol and fatty foods. Increase your energy expenditure through exercise or movement. The result is that you *will* lose weight.

Balance the physical objects in your space in the same way. If you have an excess of stuff, then you need to:

- *Reduce* the amount of stuff you bring into your life. Stop collecting brochures, junk mail, old clothes your mother gives you; stop buying things on sale when you don't have a need for the item, and so on.
- *Increase* the amount of stuff you let go from your life. Start taking more things to the op shop; cancel subscriptions to newsletters and catalogues you don't read; throw out broken, outdated and unloved items; and use the delete key.

A simple example: a new shirt is purchased, an old shirt let go. Build this kind of behaviour into your day-to-day life and the balance will automatically start to happen.

Truths: staying focused

'Focus: You can be smart, well-read, creative and knowledgeable, but none of it is any use if your mind isn't on the job.'

New Scientist magazine

You might be reasonably skilled at being organised. You might have read all the books and have every organising product known to humankind. But you don't finish anything, or you have 200 things on the go at any given time. You might call yourself 'creative'. But are you productive?

Focus means knowing what's important and what's not. Focus means planning, starting, doing and completing one thing at a time. Busy is good; fractured is not. A lack of focus will hinder your progress.

So how to improve the situation? Here are a few strategies:

- *Improve your health and environment.* Make sure you have a good balance of exercise, nutritious food and adequate sleep. Don't underestimate the power of the simple things.
- *Pay attention.* James Arthur Ray says, 'Energy goes where attention flows'. This is so true! With a little practice, you can improve your concentration and focus. If you find your thoughts wandering, stop yourself and bring your thoughts back to the task at hand. Like any habit, you will find the more you do this, the easier it gets. Meditation may help you too.
- *Minimise distractions.* Shut the door, take the phone off the hook and put up a 'do not disturb' sign, even if it's only for 10 minutes so you can simply finish something you've started. A kitchen timer is a

great tool too: you can decide how long to spend and concentrate until a task is done. Five-, 10- and 15-minute blocks work a treat.

- *Avoid multitasking.* Very few people are skilled enough to multitask with a high level of accuracy. Work out what is at the top of your list and prioritise accordingly. Again, use the numbers game: what 20 per cent of the things that you have on the go *really* matter? Focus on the top part of your list and you will find the tasks are completed more easily. Or ask yourself: what's the best use of my time *right now*?

Less is more.

Three things I would like to focus more on are

1 _____

2 _____

3 _____

Three things that I am not going to focus on are

1 _____

2 _____

3 _____

Tip

Learn to say 'no'. If you are a person who is constantly called upon to do things and you're already overextended or feel uncomfortable saying 'no', try this technique. The next time someone asks something of you, say, 'Can I give you an answer tomorrow?' This gives you a buffer to decide if you really are in a position to commit.

Truths: taking time

It takes time to be organised. And it's proportionate: the busier you are, the more time you need to devote to organising. Saying that you 'don't have time' or that you're 'too busy' is a very popular excuse. *Make the time.* If you are suffering because of a lack of organisation, you need to make time to get on top of things. Remember the old saying 'If you want something done, ask a busy person'? Busy people are often organised people. The more they do, the more organised they know they have to be. Reprioritise. Move organising time up your list of things to do.

You can't get organised once. Like learning Italian or getting fit, you need to make time for it on a regular basis. How do you spend your time? Do you waste time? Do you watch a lot of television? Chatter too much? Faff around? Surf the internet when you don't need to? Be aware of how you *really* spend your time. Keep a time diary, wear a watch (check it often) or use an eggtimer.

I resolve to spend more time getting organised by spending less time on the following:

1 _____

2 _____

3 _____

Truths: the value in routine

Routine sounds boring; it sounds rigid, and way too hard. Wrong. There's great value in routine. Routine, simply put, is planning. Knowing that you have to put the rubbish bins out on Sunday night means the rubbish is collected. Knowing your BAS is due on the 28th of the month means that you allow time to prepare and that your tax is paid on time with no late fees. Both of these tasks are planned for and happen routinely.

The truth is that organised people do not have the organising fairies visit. Organised people spend time planning and very often have routines in place. They invest today to make life easier tomorrow.

The more routine you have, the more efficient you are likely to be. Think about the regular things in your life that need taking care of, like having your hair cut, your car serviced, your tax return prepared. Generally, these things happen because you've planned to do them. So take this concept further by planning to deal with all the other things in your life. Start building a plan – some kind of routine – with the tasks in your life.

- Make a regular time – once a week at a minimum – to maintain your paper (all those piles that grow on the kitchen bench or desktop). Make a regular time to rehang and fold the clothes you've not put away.

- It's a good idea to build on existing routines. You might, for example, put away clean dishes while the kettle boils in the morning, or sort and file your emails on the same day as a weekly meeting.
- Use the changes in daylight-savings time to prompt annual tasks, such as clearing out a storage area or organising your office and returning any personal items home. That's two organising bees a year.

The more frequently you perform a routine, the less you will have to do. Sorting a month's worth of paper is going to take four times as long as sorting a weekly pile. Common sense? Yes. Rewarding? Yes. Difficult to achieve? No. It's a simple technique that, if used *consistently*, will give you excellent results.

It might sound boring, but there's nothing more liberating than the freedom that comes from routine. It means you're now free to spend your time and energy doing the stuff you really want to do.

In order to be more organised, a new routine I will build into my life will be

_____

_____

_____

_____

_____

_____

Techniques: setting goals

People who achieve results usually set goals. They're not always written down, but if you do take the time to write them down, you will be able to check back on them (accountability). Writing them down also means you will be *very clear* about what you are trying to achieve. Goal setting is not difficult when you know how. The best goals have structure. They are SMART goals. They are:

- specific
- measurable
- achievable
- realistic
- timed.

To understand SMART goals, let's look at a goal that doesn't apply the SMART rules: 'My goal is to get fit'. This statement is far too broad. How fit is fit? How will your fitness be measured before and after? How long will it take to get fit? Are you capable of achieving the fitness you desire? As you can see, giving structure to your goals and applying the SMART principles are crucial to success.

Be aware that setting yourself too many goals is a recipe for failure. So is setting goals that are too big. If you are new to setting goals (or feel you have failed at goal setting in the past), just start with one goal and make it small. Trying to create too much change at once is often overwhelming, so take it slowly and gently. A simple goal to start with could be trying one organising recipe a week.

Even for small successes, celebrate the achievement of your goals. Promise yourself a reward for completing each task, or for finishing the whole job. Your reward might be something as simple as a coffee and sticky bun for finishing a task, or an evening soak in the bath after spending the whole afternoon getting the office sorted. Organising can be mentally and physically tiring, particularly if you're not used to it, so make sure you allow for some 'you' time in your organising schedule.

Techniques: sorting

If you're faced with disarray, you need to start sorting. Sorting involves taking a jumbled mess – a 'mixed bag' – and creating new categories. The trick with sorting is to always use as few categories as possible. The biggest mistake you can make is to create too many new categories. I think no more than four or five categories at any time is the way to go. Too many categories mean too many choices, and that means decision making is harder.

For example, if you're sorting wool and you start with a big box of many different shades, you don't want to have to separate that into the thirty or more different colours that are represented in the box. It's too hard to process with that many choices, and our brain gets confused. Fewer choices make segmentation easy. A good approach to the coloured wool problem would be to sort the piles something like this:

- reds and pinks
- greens and blues
- browns and yellows
- neutrals.

Sorting, and retrieval, suddenly becomes easier.

If you want to take things further, a clever technique is simply to sort them again by doing a second round of sorting – the reds and pinks category might comprise six or eight different shades, styles or thicknesses. It's a quick method that can be done in stages. The more you do it, the better you'll get. A simple system makes processing anything so much more manageable.

● Editing

Editing is a big part of organising. It's about selecting the best and letting the not-so-good go. Professional photographers are skilled editors. They take a large volume of work and whittle it down to a few good shots. Let's say they photograph thirty images: they might end up with only two or three stunning shots out of that much work.

Film editors edit raw footage to make a stronger film. They snip thirty seconds here and thirty seconds there to create a better and tighter film. Less information (less stuff) means more clarity and a better end product.

Life is like this. There's lots of stuff that doesn't matter: things you're 'going to do'; outdated, broken or not-so-good stuff. If you constantly edit the stuff in your life, you'll stay organised. Give some thought to what's truly special. Be an editor every day. Constantly reassess and you'll find that the things that don't matter easily slip away.

Techniques: visual clarity

> 'Form follows function' – that has been misunderstood.
> Form and function should be joined in spiritual union.
>
> Frank Lloyd Wright

Clutter or a jumbled tangle of stuff can be really ugly. It can certainly be visually overwhelming, which in turn simply confuses your brain. Visual clarity means having some clean lines and some space for your eye to rest. A good example of achieving visual clarity is making the bed in the morning. Even if there are some clothes not put away or some books and magazines lying around, the made bed provides visual clarity. Putting away washed dishes will give you clarity. A well-labelled filing cabinet will give you visual clarity. A desktop clear of papers and stationery gives visual clarity.

The main benefit of visual clarity is that you can *focus* on what remains. So, if you're organising your office, first clear the desktop before you begin sorting. You will find it much easier to work that way. Spending five minutes putting things away means you have a clear work space and are less likely to feel overwhelmed.

Visual clarity can often involve repetition too. Repetition can be something as simple as a row of books of a similar size, three chairs placed together, or neat rows of drinking glasses. Repetition is an extremely powerful design tool and frequently provides visual clarity. It also means you can actually work with *less*. For example, when decorating, using just two colours and repeating those colours in various shades can be far more effective than using a complex palette of multiple colours.

Art directing

When I worked in advertising and as a photographic stylist, I secretly wanted to be an art director. An art director is someone who controls the creative look of a space, directing its composition, scale, texture and the overall look and feel.

Play art director in your space as you get organised. What elements do you have an excess of? Is everything made from timber? Do you have lots of 'little things' – small bookcases, small tables, small containers? A good art director will ensure there's a balance of elements and that the overall look and feel are harmonious. A good 'look and feel' can mean something as simple as colour blocking (placing like colours together) or including a tall plant to balance a high ceiling. Art directing is often about balance. Another good way of achieving the right look and feel is to mix pretty and practical objects – a picture frame next to books, a candle near a mirror, a trinket box next to a tumbler of pens. Use interesting containers, and always check the kitchen for any unique and infrequently used storage items. Op shops and markets are a great source of funky, colourful items. Experiment and you'll soon work out which containers you like and why.

Creative types

There's a myth that becoming organised means you will lose your creativity. Traditionally, we creative types haven't been known for our organisation skills. As well as having a different head space (random, ramshackle, innovative), we often harbour an underlying fear that being organised – or worse, visually neat – will take away our creativity. That fear is unfounded. Being organised and efficient is conducive to your creative pursuits. It liberates your mind and space, and it allows you the joyous freedom to create whenever the mood strikes.

Order can be empowering. It provides visual clarity, which enables you to see what you've got and to lay your hands on it. It's about referencing and using what you have. Visual clarity can also provide inspiration of the best kind: that sense of having things under control. Consider your resources and your current effectiveness. Allow things to flow, and work as you normally do, but put some damned good infrastructure in place and you will fly.

Techniques: disposal

There are loads of ways for you to dispose of your unwanted goods. Wherever possible, try to recycle, because these days it's really easy and we have only limited resources on this earth. Always remember to:

- recycle
- reduce
- reuse.

Landfill can be avoided. Don't take the promotional show bags with samples you will never use. Don't buy things on sale because they 'might' be useful or are cheap. It's all landfill, so don't contribute to creating it.

Don't get hung up on selling things. Bear in mind that selling anything – whether it's at a garage sale or on eBay – takes time, effort and focus. Don't say you're going to do it and then fail to make it happen. If it's important enough to sell, make sure you plan it through and complete the task. Don't leave that spare printer in the office cupboard for so long that it becomes obsolete.

Sometimes when you've got a lot of sorting to do, it's better just to use the rubbish or recycling bin rather than create more work for yourself. The no-brainers include old magazines (doctors' surgeries and op shops really don't want them), puzzles with pieces missing, tools or machines with missing parts that are difficult to replace. The keys here are decisiveness and speed. Get on with it or get over it. Just don't hang on to it!

Once you've made the decision to dispose of something, make sure you get rid of it fast. Try:

- www.freecycle.org
- your local op shop
- friends and family
- eBay
- your local second-hand store or pawn shop
- the rubbish tip (as a last resort). Many tips now have their own stores for re-selling unwanted goods.

It's important to remember that if you do *anything* other than chuck it out (or recycle it in the bin), it will take you time and energy to find it a good home. Are you prepared to follow this though? If you are, make time, and give yourself a deadline to get rid of it.

Techniques: labelling

Labelling is a crucial part of being organised. It's not so much about aesthetics, but more about information. A label is information. Any kind of label will save you time since you won't need to revisit the contents later or rely on memory.

Be mindful that labelling alone *does not* make you organised. It's a common misconception. Labelling is merely a tool to aid organisation.

Some different types of labels are:

- labelmaker labels – the schmick version that looks great
- texta labelling – perfect for labelling cardboard boxes
- sticky notes – great temporary labelling for a 'work in progress' and ideal before you sign off on titles or categories.

Labelling things clearly and concisely the first time will save you time and money. It's all very well having a filing cabinet full of stuff, but not if you can't find what you need in five seconds or less. Consider placing a summary of your files at the front of each drawer. You'll know immediately which files are in which drawers.

Tip

Label the foil side of blister-pack medications with a texta for each day of the week: 'M' for Monday, 'T' for Tuesday, and so on. For medication taken twice daily, simply write the letter twice. Easy!

Techniques: maintenance

One of the secrets to being organised is maintenance. You can't get organised just once. Life undoes things. That's natural and normal.

Implementing systems for maintenance will ensure you stay organised. Make time and plan to maintain the stuff in your life. Clear your desktop; do some filing; put away tools and equipment after you've used them. Plan time to cull your filing cabinet; take down the Christmas decorations and revisit things stored at the top of the wardrobe or in the shed. Ensure all your files are clearly labelled, and make the time to deal with clothes at the end of the season. Make it routine to unpack your bag completely as soon as you get back from holidays or a business trip. Make it your goal to clear the decks on a regular basis, and make it your goal to complete the job 100 per cent. It's a feel-good moment when you're done.

One of the simplest maintenance tips is: *don't put it down; put it away!* This simple rule keeps any space looking fresh and clutter-free. It also means you'll find the item you want when you want it.

3 Recipes

You're now ready to start organising. A few tips before you begin:

- The time frames quoted in these recipes are *an indication only* – you may find that your unique situation requires more time, but don't be discouraged! Organising can be done in stages; in fact, it's very unusual to go from 'disorder' to 'order' in one session. When people ask me, 'How long will it take?', I ask them, 'How long is a piece of string?' Everyone is very different, but remember that any time you spend getting organised is time well spent.
- As you would with a cooking recipe, gather all your tools and equipment in one place. Try to work uninterrupted.
- Finally, make sure you clear up when you're finished. Put the rubbish out; put away tools and equipment; take your recycling to the bin. Distribute items to charity or friends as soon as possible. Clearing the decks will really give you a sense of completion. And, importantly, reward yourself when you're done.

Recipes can be used again and again, or in combination with other recipes; for example, you might use four or five paper recipes that suit your style of organising best. Mix it up!

Work

Wouldn't it be great to be more efficient at work – to have the kind of productive work days that allow you truly to relax in your life outside of the office, rather than worrying about all the tasks and projects you have to do or are pulling off? For me, a good day is a productive day. With a bit of practice, you can have these kinds of productive days too. It just requires getting things into order and taking care of what you've got.

The ultimate desk layout

The way your desk is set up is crucial to your productivity, efficiency and wellbeing, whether you're at home or at work, a sole trader or part of a large organisation, managing household paperwork, working as part of a support network (for instance, in an administrative role) or studying.

Make sure you work in a well-lit area, free from glare from your computer screen. Task lighting in the form of a desk lamp will ensure you can work comfortably. Natural light is important too, as is fresh air to give you a sense of wellbeing and comfort. If your working space is small – or the room your desk occupies is a shared space – you will need to be frugal and pare your desktop items back to only the essentials. It's likely that you use only 20 per cent of your tools and resources on a daily basis. Keep the essentials close at hand and be ruthless with the rest. Your space will immediately look larger as a result.

You will need
- an hour or more
- your desk space and related items (furniture and contents)
- rubbish and recycling bins
- an empty cardboard carton for op shop items

Desktop for working, not storing

Current projects/ work in progress

If you are right-handed and use a mouse, the telephone is best on the left-hand side of the computer

Stationery lives here

Most commonly used files

Most valuable space (often neglected). Use to store diary, phone book and other frequently used tools

Just a few pens!

Task lighting

Keep printer close at hand

Ideal spot to 'process' paper; for example, bills to pay

Commonly used resources

Natural light and fresh air

Your best friend: the bin

Store financial paperwork or lesser accessed items here

Archives

Method

1   Relocate your desk away from traffic areas.

2   Clear everything off your desk and off any shelves in the immediate area. Leave organising your drawers (the minutiae) until last.

3   Culling as you go, first return the most commonly used items to your desktop. This is usually your computer, keyboard and mouse, pencil cup, telephone and any files or reference materials used on a daily basis.

4   Then return secondary items: your printer, scanner, rubbish bin and so on. Any files that have to be kept but that are not used for working should be archived.

Tips

✓   Clear your desk at the end of each working day (maintenance). This contributes to visual clarity and provides a 'fresh start' when you sit down to work the next time. It's not inspiring to walk into a space in which mess and clutter dominate the horizontal surfaces. It will make you feel out of control. And it will not make you want to work. Clutter, particularly visual clutter, can be distracting. Clear the decks so that you can be more in control and feel confident as you start your working day.

✓   Keep the balance between messy productivity and an occasional 'clearing of the decks'.

✓   Check the ergonomics of your set-up. Your computer should be directly in front of you as you work; your elbows should be at right angles and your computer screen an arm's length away. Your mouse and keyboard should always be on the same level – the same horizontal surface.

✓   Glare from the screen can cause headaches and eye strain, so make sure your computer is in a position that avoids glaring, and take regular breaks from your computer-based work.

- ✓ Take frequent breaks – at least one an hour. Stand up, wriggle your arms and shake your legs. Gently stretch your neck from side to side. Touch your toes. Fetch a drink, check your letterbox if you work from home, or walk around the garden or outside for five minutes.
- ✓ Do not underestimate the importance of physical comfort. Make sure your chair is decent and that you feel well supported – particularly on your lumbar, which is in the lower back.
- ✓ Some of these ergonomic tips might sound irrelevant, but if ignored, the consequences can negatively influence your productivity, health and comfort.
- ✓ As a general rule, try not to have your back to the door, so you know when someone enters the room, and your work remains private.

Digital: files

A place for everything and everything in its place. The tricks here are to group like objects together and to make friends with your delete key.

You will need
- between 15 minutes and an hour – anything longer than an hour will give you brain drain, so digital organising is best done in chunks
- your computer
- random digital files

Method
1   If you haven't already done so, create folders (or directories) to house your files. If you already have folders, make sure they are sorted into no more than four or five main categories. Use the filing map recipe (on page 88) to work out what you're keeping, and create appropriate headings for your main categories. Subcategories can be addressed later; focus on the bigger picture and don't get lost in detail, otherwise your progress will be slow. If you feel confident and/or have a large number of files that are related, create subcategories as you go.

2 Tighten up your existing folders by renaming and collating them *before* you sort anything that's not already filed. You can bunch anything not filed (a 'mixed bag') into a folder called 'filing' to process after you've worked out your bigger picture.

3 Make a note on paper of any very large folders that will need further sorting – such as any files labelled 'miscellaneous' – as you can also come back to these.

Tips

✓ Don't keep the original files on your desktop. Instead, use aliases to create a link to frequently used files. This ensures that the original always remains in the correct place. Treat your digital desktop just like your physical one: free from anything you're not actually working on.

✓ Don't worry if your files need a lot of attention. Keep your eye on the bigger picture.

✓ Don't forget: you can use the 'search' or 'find' button.

Backing up

Backing up is crucial to prevent loss of data. Imagine that you run a business. What will you do if your computer is stolen and you have no backup? Or what if you have a backup, but it's very old and incomplete? Or what if it is also stolen with the computer? What if you religiously back up (albeit not that often) but you've never actually tested it to see if it *works*? The best and most concise overview of computer backup can be found at www.taobackup.com.

Digital: email

Treat email much as you would paper. Digital clutter can be just as detrimental as physical clutter.

You will need

- Between 15 minutes and an hour – anything longer than an hour will give you brain drain, so digital organising is best done in chunks
- your computer
- random emails

Method

1 Sometimes you're better off just starting again with a new system. For example, if you have a huge backlog of email – say you have 3000 emails in your inbox – simply archive them in a folder called 'email pre 1.1.07' and start afresh with an empty box and a new system. It's sometimes more efficient to start again than sort old information.

2 Start by archiving anything outdated that you absolutely have to keep. A folder called 'archives' is sufficient.

3 Flag any emails that are crucial and referred to often.

4 Any emails that require action should remain in your inbox. You should only file 'active' emails in a folder if you have made a written note elsewhere of the job that needs doing. Once it's filed, you won't remember what you have to work on or attend to.

Tips

✓ Use filters or rules. These will automatically sort your mail into specific folders. A word of caution though: filtering everything means you must be able to keep tabs on emails that require action, so remember to mark them as 'unread' if they still need your attention.

✓ Avoid multiple systems. Even if your method is less than perfect, one system is better than two (or none).

✓ Use the phone! Email can be a huge time-waster, so pick up the phone and speak to the person and you might find that you avoid lots of back-and-forthing.

✓ Keep your address book current. Back it up.

Books and media

Part of the trick here is setting a boundary and containing your resources within a bookcase or similar storage system. You might be one of those people who cannot possibly part with a single book, CD or vinyl record, and that's fine. But disorder and an absence of logical storage systems will mean you probably can't find what you need and are at risk of double-buying. Worse, you waste time looking for the item you want.

Have a minor cull as you go. Ask yourself, 'Would I burst if I no longer owned this book?' Your response to this question is the litmus test for ownership. Keep only what you're really passionate about. Even if you can't throw out a single item, a reorganisation means you'll be better acquainted with the titles you do own.

Respect what you own. Poorly housing your collections will not protect your investment.

You will need

- 60 minutes or more
- books, CDs or vinyl records
- ample shelves

Method

1 Gather all your media in one place. If you already have bookshelves, first remove some of the books from the shelves so that you have some empty space to plug into. Wipe down the shelves as you go.

2 Decide how you would like your books to be categorised – I recommend categorising by genre. For example, books are often best sorted like they are in a bookstore or library: fiction, travel (include maps and street directories and even your passport here), reference, cooking, coffee-table books and so on. I've seen books sorted by the colour of the spine, but I can't recommend this approach unless you have a huge number of colourful books and an unbelievable memory. For CDs, a genre or alphabetical approach works best. My vinyl records are organised by genre, but the genres are chronological too as they reflect my musical interests over a period of time.

3 Whatever categories you choose, be consistent.

4 Once you've sorted into your main categories, return your books to the shelves, keeping the most frequently used genres at eye level or just below. Do not overcrowd your shelves! Having enough room to put items away easily is crucial. Room for the future is necessary.

Tips

✓ Always store books vertically unless they are very small or very large, in which case you can stack them horizontally (a design trick). If necessary, use bookends or something with a little weight and height (a small pot plant) to keep your books upright.

✓ The 'out' list:

✗ *books:* old uni texts; crappy paperbacks you bought at a garage sale and have never read; equipment manuals for things you no longer own

✗ *CDs:* anything you used to love but have played so much that you can't bear to hear it again; anything you bought at a garage sale and never listened to; anything you bought cheap at a gig to be polite and because it seemed like a good idea at the time; anything you just don't love or haven't played in the past year

✗ *vinyl:* anything that is so scratched or damaged that you won't play it any more; any gifts or freebies you have received and are ambivalent about; any vinyl you keep seeing in second-hand stores (indicating that no one wants it).

✓ Empty CD jewel cases work a treat as dividers. Using sturdy labels, you can create visual markers to divide your collection. Make sure the labels extend out from the edge and there you have it: instant indexing.

✓ Vinyl records fit perfectly into IKEA's EXPEDIT shelves, which have three sizes (approximately 1.5 metres square or 1.8 metres square), plus a half size (approximately 1.5 x 0.8 metres). These versatile shelves also work a treat as a room divider.

- ✓ Book Darts or 3M Post-it durable index tabs work much better than bookmarks or regular sticky labels for flagging important information. They are sturdier, and you can flag a specific line of text with accuracy. They are great for students or for anyone working in an information-rich field (such as law).
- ✓ Bookplates are small self-adhesive stickers that you stick on the inside front covers of your books to label them as yours. They were first used when books were rare and precious. If you have loads of books, and often lend them, these are a great idea, particularly for kids' books. At the very least, write your name inside the cover.
- ✓ If you lend books and CDs, keep a small notebook with your collection to note the date and person you lent the item to. Three months is a reasonable term to loan an item; any longer than that and you might not see it again. Make sure the borrower knows the terms on which you are lending. Be a good borrower by making sure you have made a note of what you've borrowed, from whom and when. Return the item promptly, even if it is unread – it's good manners.
- ✓ Cover your most valuable or most frequently used books with clear plastic to protect them. Art supplies stores or archivists sell plastic by the metre. For vinyl, clear plastic record sleeves also do the trick. You've spent good money on the item, so protect your investment – your return if reselling will be better too. And replace any dodgy jewel cases on your CDs – there's nothing more annoying than the jewel case falling apart when you pick it up.
- ✓ Use them or lose them! Sorting your collection and organising it periodically should reacquaint you with titles you forgot you had, prompting you to enjoy them again.

✓ If your shelving is too deep in height, consider adding further shelves to create more horizontal space.

✓ All collections benefit from the setting of boundaries. If you don't set a boundary, at what point do you stop? And how do you refine the quality of your stuff? Collecting a certain genre, author or topic gives a sense of satisfaction as you expand the collection, and there is usually an 'end' point. Or apply the 'new title in, old title out' principle. Imagine owning your favourite 100 albums of all time – a bit like *Desert Island Discs*. Or imagine the satisfaction of owning the first editions of a much-loved author. *Volume alone doesn't make a good library.*

✓ Think 'library': a stepladder will give you access to titles stored up high, and it works particularly well for custom built-in shelving.

CD spindle

A CD spindle is a great way to clean up cumbersome and ever-multiplying CDs. It's perfect for discs that don't need a cover, such as software and 'home burns' like backup, music and photo CDs. Use this recipe as a categorising tool and compact storage solution. No more 'chaosification'!

You will need

- 45 minutes per spindle
- random CDs
- a CD spindle (the kind that blank CDs come on). Ask your local IT geek if you don't have one
- stiff card (an old manila folder is perfect)
- fine tipped texta
- scissors
- a rubbish bin
- a pencil, eraser, sharpener and ruler

Method

1 Discard all the CD covers. View and label any unlabelled CDs.
2 Sort your CDs into main categories, such as:
   - music
   - backup
   - software
   - photos.

3   Place a CD on the card and trace around it. Then trace a small tab approx 1 centimetre x 3.5 centimetres. Try to keep the tab reasonably small so that the lid of the spindle will go back on.

4   Cut out the cardboard divider and label the tabs with a fine texta or thick pen according to your main categories.

5   Place the CDs on the spindle according to category. Put them in chronological order if appropriate, making sure the most recent CDs are on the top, and separate each category with a cardboard divider as you go.

Tips

✓   Flag important CDs with a small sticky note – for example, 'business plan 21/2/07 backup', 'Big Day Out 2006' or 'party mix MP3s'.

✓   This is a great system for regular burns, like backup disks. Simply place the most recent CD on top and you're organised.

Cable wrangling

A tangled mess of cables is unsightly and confusing. Take the time to sort your office or audiovisual cabling now. Getting things in order makes for an easier life: no more stress when it's time to unplug the printer; no more resetting the clock on the DVD player when all you meant to do was a bit of vacuuming; no more 'Which cable is this from?'; no desperate untangling when you want to move the printer.

No matter what size your set-up is, take a professional approach to organising your cables. Gaffers, musicians and IT geeks are experts at wrangling cables, and even 'wrapping' cables (rolling them up) is done in a particular way. They're great at creating order

75

and keeping things safe. I'm a bit of a geek and have wrapped a few cables in my time working in film and video, so let me show you how easy it is to develop impressive wrangling skills.

You will need

- 15–30 minutes
- a mess of cables
- cable ties
- your preferred labelling tool (or tools)

Method

1   Decide on the location of your equipment. Does anything need reconfiguring? Do it now.
2   Turn off all appliances and unplug everything at the power socket. If you're keen, take the opportunity to wipe dust away underneath the appliance and use a clean paintbrush to flick away dust from the back and from any other tricky crevices.
3   Carefully untangle all cords.
4   Label the plugs with the appliance name. If the cable can also be removed from the actual appliance (for instance, from a computer screen), label the plug at both ends. Labels can be tape and paper (not such a long-life span), flags, labelmaker labels or fine-tipped texta or whiteout pen marked directly onto the plug itself. If you mark the plug directly, first make sure that you are writing on the top edge of the plug; you will need to hold it with the pins in the right direction.
5   Now 'track' your cables. For example, a printer and a computer that sit side by side and that are plugged into the same wall can have their cables laid together and held in place with Velcro cable straps

or cable tie. *Caution*: never loop excess cables on plugged-in appliances as this can cause overheating, subsequent shortages and possibly fire. Looping lengths of cable can actually increase the voltage. *Never* fix cable ties too tightly; you should still be able to slide the cables within the tie.

6　Run cables at the back of a desk or along a wall. Fix cable ties at convenient points like the edge of a desk – a second Velcro tie or hook onto the desk will often allow for further concealment.

Tips

✓　Invest in bigger GPOs (general power outlets) Four sockets are the bare minimum for offices, kitchens and audiovisual set-ups. Also consider buying powerboards with extra space between sockets for all those appliances with fat adaptors. Label the adaptor too

✓　Remove any excess extension leads or double adaptors. Excess leads that are not in use can be looped and secured with sturdy string or an old shoelace: tie to the socket end of the lead first before securing the loop.

✓　Consider using cable wraps or clips from cableorganizer.com/cableties-wrap-clips. These Velcro critters are similar to the devices that are often provided with mobile phone chargers to keep the cables neat and contained.

✓　Do you want to get the most out of your equipment and to use it efficiently? Make the time to read the manual. Flag any important pages.

✓　At www.kableflags.com.au, you can purchase nifty little rubber flags that enable you to label your electrical plugs with ease. They come in a pack or individually.

Paper

Paper can be a burden. Lots of little bits of paper very quickly add up to one big, fat office, filing cabinet or desk. You might have piles of paper, and the layers of documents covering your horizontal surfaces might be reminiscent of geological strata dating back to the Neolithic period. You might also be using the floor. Paper is not complicated. It's only hard work when you keep *everything*. It's important that you *keep only what counts*.

Less is best

Any file with fewer than three pieces of paper does not deserve its own file. You'll end up with too many categories otherwise. (The exception to this rule is when you know the file is going to grow – a new bank account, for instance, warrants its own file.) You're better off taking those three pieces, clipping them together or placing them in a plastic sleeve or pocket, labelling them and including them in a file that has a broader title. For example, let's say you have a newspaper cutting about a course you would like to do for your professional development (one piece of paper). You then make a telephone enquiry and the course coordinator sends you a brochure that includes the registration form (two pieces of paper). After perusing the information and checking – and pencilling – the dates in your diary, you decide to take the course. So you post off the registration form and fee. They send a confirmation letter by return (three pieces of paper). Until you actually begin the course, or begin collecting other reference and research materials, these pieces of paper could live within another file – perhaps a folder called 'professional development'. The larger file might include subcategories such as:

- CV
- current job applications
- old job applications
- courses I'd like to do
- courses I've done.

Once the course is under way, you can create a whole new file for your desktop, as the paper related to that course becomes a 'work in progress' (an ongoing project). You may even end up with a folder that houses all of your course material, with subcategories such as:

- course overview
- current assignments
- completed assignments
- class notes
- research and reference materials
- administration (where the application forms and course information could be housed).

Eventually, when the course is complete, you could archive this folder. After a period of time, you would probably discard most paper other than the certificate you earned.

Get the idea? Always look at the broader category before starting a new file. Make sure you allow your files to grow or change as your paper does.

Categories and colour coding

Colour coding is generally not a good idea. The reason for this is that most people use too many colours. You do not want to be 'tied' to having multiple coloured pens, folders or suspension files. It's just not always that convenient. Colour coding doesn't allow for an infinite number of categories, and it can quickly become confusing, expensive and time-consuming to maintain.

Having said that, a simple colour coding system, using between two and four colours, can work. For a home-based business, you might use something as simple as green folders for work and white folders for personal records. To take things a step further, you could use a second system to colour code your labels. (Don't forget that you can use colour coding for digital files too.)

Tips

✓ Allow your filing to evolve. If you are setting up something from scratch, write your labels in pencil until you have lived with the new system for a month or so; this allows you to finetune it.

✓ If you find yourself creating a 'miscellaneous' category, try again. The term 'miscellaneous' is far too broad, and every item you're filing could come under a specific heading.

✓ Reassessing your paper files from time to time will ensure the *relevance* and *currency* of what you're keeping.

✓ The most important question you need to ask yourself when organising your paper is 'What's the worst that could happen if I throw it away?'

✓ Invest in a shredder. Shred daily. Recycle the shredding in the cat litter tray, the compost or the recycling bin.

✓ Recycle A4 paper into A5 pads by ripping them in half with a metal ruler or taking them to a printer's for guillotining. A fold-back bulldog clip allows the paper to be hung from a hook.

✓ Keep all your paper in one place, not multiple locations.

Sorting: the four Fs

This is a super-fast way to sort your paper and get organised. It's a decision-making tool. It's about *sorting* – not about acting on anything. Unless it will save a life, don't act on anything straightaway; just focus on the bigger picture. If you have many piles of paper to sort, allow 15–30 minutes per batch. The more rubbish you find, the faster it will be. As a very rough guide, a 10-centimetre pile of unsorted paper should take about 20 minutes to process.

You will need

- 20 minutes or more
- unsorted paper
- three cardboard cartons (any kind)
- a rubbish or recycling bin
- a stapler
- a texta
- an Esselte Nalclip dispenser and fasteners
- approximately 1.5 metres x 1.5 metres of floor space or a large table

Finish it

Forward it

File it

Flick it

Method

1 If you're able, work on the floor. Label each of your four boxes: **'finish it'**, **'forward it'**, **'file it'** and **'flick it'**. (The 'flick it' container can be a big rubbish bin.)

2 Place the boxes in an arc around you. Make sure the 'flick it' container is closest to you.

3 Grab a pile of paper and put the pile right in front of you. If you have lots of piles, process them in batches that are each approximately 10–15 centimetres thick.

4 Take the top piece of paper and decide which of the four piles to put it in.

5 Repeat until all the paper is sorted.

Tips

✓ Make friends with your rubbish bin!

✓ Any document in an envelope should be removed and opened; do not leave it folded up.

✓ Use your stapler or Esselte Nalclip fasteners to keep like items together; for example, a two-page letter, multiple pages of a bill.

✓ Stay focused on the task at hand, and make a decision about one piece of paper before moving on to the next.

✓ Don't have a 'not sure' pile – I promise that *every* piece of paper you own will fall under one of the four categories listed above.

✓ Always take paper from the top of the pile. Handle each piece of paper only once when making decisions.

✓ Save money by making sure you keep all your claimable health fund and/or Medicare receipts safely in one place. Don't let them get lost in a sea of paper! A small drawer or large envelope works a treat.

Submit all your receipts once a year and you'll have your own savings plan for a weekend away or special treat.

✓ Keep only what *really* counts.
✓ When you're done, recycle your paper and/or shred anything that is of a sensitive nature.

The four Fs

1   Finish it.

This category is for anything that is a work in progress. It includes *current* things like:

- bills to pay
- work to do
- education or professional development (such as an assignment or study materials)
- personal projects (for example, learning Italian)
- vouchers
- upcoming events (such as researching a holiday)
- any forms to fill out
- drafts of letters
- health claim refunds
- unchecked lottery tickets
- creative projects on the go
- a tax return in progress
- unwritten birthday cards
- financial reconciliations
- receipts for items to be returned.

2 Forward it.

This is for the stuff that's about to leave your space. It's paper that doesn't belong to you. It's things like:

- forms you've filled out
- paper belonging to someone else (for example, kids' homework)
- paper you've borrowed (such as a copy of an article)
- anything that is no longer useful to you but that you know is of value to someone else.

3 File it.

This is likely to be the largest pile and will contain all the documentation you need to file for future reference. This category includes only items you absolutely have to keep. Financial documentation like old electricity bills should only be kept for twelve months or less unless it's tax-related. This category includes things like:

- bank statements
- paid bills
- credit card statements
- mortgage or loan information
- donation receipts
- investment information
- receipts for major purchases
- memberships
- insurance paperwork
- employment contracts
- business cards
- professional resources
- renovation documentation
- health records

- prescriptions (these can be kept with your medications or in a file)
- warranties
- equipment manuals
- academic certificates
- your will, marriage and birth certificate
- entertainment information
- recipes
- takeaway menus
- information on things you want to buy
- articles cut from the paper
- information on pets
- travel information
- maps
- personal development
- spiritual interests
- study, school or university information and materials
- kids' entertainment information
- loyalty programs
- sporting information
- motor vehicle registration and other documentation
- creative ideas
- correspondence
- memorabilia (such as letters, certificates and so on).

4   **Flick it.**

Flick it! Chuck it out! This will be one of the biggest piles of paper and should include anything you're not sure about – *if in doubt, chuck it out*. If you can replace the paper (for instance, a print-out from a website or a brochure for something you 'might' do), get rid of it *now*. This pile includes things like:

- out-of-date information
- kids' artwork
- unwanted receipts
- old cards and letters
- paid bills (unless you need them for your tax records)
- junk mail
- loyalty program brochures
- out-of-date price lists
- stationery (unless it is in mint condition)
- newspapers
- magazines
- information on past events
- newsletters
- gym timetables that you never use.

Sorting: filing map

When you think about organising your paper, do you think, 'Well, it could be filed in any one of fifty different places?' No wonder filing seems like such a chore. The easiest way to manage paper is to break it down. The secret is to have *fewer* categories. A good way to achieve this is to create a filing map – a map of where your paper lives. Your filing map applies to both digital and paper files.

You will need
- 15 minutes or more
- a pen
- blank A4 paper

Method
1   Start by identifying just three or four primary categories. This allows for easy filing and instant access. Let's say you're running a small business that offers cleaning. The headings for your filing map might look like this:

Accounts	Infrastructure	Clients	Marketing

Every piece of paper you file will come under one of these four categories.

2 From here, you can flesh out the categories by creating secondary levels. For a cleaning business, it might look like this:

Accounts	Infrastructure	Clients	Marketing
Creditors	Business plan	Client files	Website
Debtors	Insurance	• Client contact details	• Mailing list
Wages	• Motor vehicle	• Client job details	• Testimonials
• Super	• Building & contents	• Signed paperwork	Special offers
• ATO information	• Public liability		Logo design & stationery
BAS	Legal		• Flyers
Reconciliations	• Trademark registration		• Magnets
Budget & business plan	• ASIC		Services info
• P&L statements	Staffing		Sales team info
• Tax returns	• Current contracts		Market research
	• Previous applicants		
	• Training		
	• Staff meetings		
	Information technology		

3 So what happens when there are various filing possibilities? What would happen if you had four or five employees who were in sales or servicing clients? You would have lots of related information like:

- wages
- training
- staff contracts
- sales team information
- staff meetings.

All this information relates to employees. Which category should it go into? *Simply making a decision and being consistent is the important thing.* Once you have a visual map of where things live, it's much clearer to file and retrieve, so it doesn't matter if your way of thinking is a little different from that of everyone else; it's best to base your filing system on how *your* brain works. For the record, my recommendation would be to *keep like with like* to avoid confusion:

- Keep all financial information together (for instance, wages under 'Accounts').
- Keep all legal information together (for instance, staff contracts under 'Legal').
- Keep all sales information together (for instance, procedures and templates under 'Marketing').
- Keep all previous applicants together (for instance, under 'Staffing').

Another way to sort would be to file everything except wages under 'Staffing'. The best approach depends somewhat on the *quantity* of paper you are keeping and on the *frequency* with which you need to access it.

4 *Use up to a maximum of four levels*, for example:

INFRASTRUCTURE (first level)
↳ Staffing (second level)
   ↳ Staff meetings (third level)
      ↳ February (fourth level)

Filing: financial paperwork and receipts

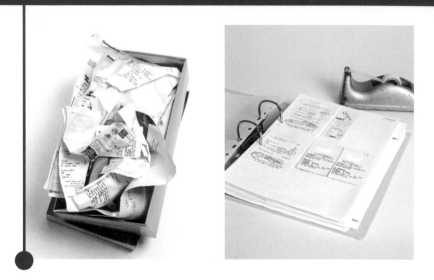

Many of us avoid sorting out fiddly financial paperwork because it's overwhelming and sounds so boring. Don't be put off! Once you know how, it's easy, and the result is truly exciting. Being on top of your financial paperwork is also very liberating. Don't leave that stuff in limbo.

This recipe shows you how to set up a simple, easy system to deal with receipts regularly. Come tax time you will feel so damned good about it. This is the stress-free way to manage the financial minutiae.

If you've got a backlog, don't forget that you can do this job in stages, so take short breaks between steps if you need to.

This recipe is best followed after you've set up your bill-paying system (see page 119).

You will need

- 30 minutes or more
- all your financial documentation, such as invoices, pay slips, receipts and superannuation documents
- sticky tape
- a pen
- a stapler
- a hole puncher
- blank A4 paper
- a lever arch folder for filing
- a spike or envelope (optional)

Method

1 Gather all your financial documentation in one place. It doesn't matter where you choose to put it: cupboard, desk drawer or shoe box. Just make sure your paperwork has a *home*. Resolve, from today onwards, not to make the mistake of having multiple homes or you will waste countless hours looking for things. Remember: *one* home for receipts.

   - Flatten out all your receipts so you can easily read them. Staple together any related receipts for the same purchase – for instance, the actual receipt and the credit card or ATM docket. Make sure all your receipts are facing up the same way.

- Highlighting the important information makes it stand out so you won't need to revisit everything on the receipt. Take a pen and circle the date, the total claimable amount and the method of payment. If it is not immediately obvious, also write what the purchase was for – for example, 'book for training', 'stationery supplies' or 'movie tickets for staff bonuses'. If you can't recall what the receipt was for, chuck it out.
- Sticky tape the receipts onto a piece of A4 paper in date order for easy handling. If it suits you, have a different page for each category – for example, stationery, travel expenses, reference materials and so on. *Or* simply place them in date order. You can also apply the same method for managing ATM receipts, deposit slips, and so on. These A4 sheets will make handling your receipts easy.

2   If you have more than two or three years' worth of paper, first sort it into financial years: 1 July 2006 – 30 June 2007, for example.

3   Sort your papers into different categories:
- income: include group certificates, pay slips, any shares, investments, interest and so on
- outgoings: include paid bills, receipts and any expenses that might be claimable (a good bookkeeper or accountant can advise you). Don't forget donations to charity, health insurance documentation, your motor vehicle log book and any other business-related travel expenses
- bank and credit card statements: include cheque stubs, deposit slips and online transfer or phone-banking receipts
- store cards and loyalty programs.

4   When you have sorted your paperwork, create a lever arch folder with dividers for each of the above categories. Take one pile at a time and place each piece of paper in date order, with the most

recent record on the top. For example, your bank statements, if issued monthly, will have 12 records: June 07, May 07, April 07 and so on. The beauty of this folder system is that once it's established, the upkeep is really simple. The most recent paperwork gets hole punched and placed within the relevant section, on the top. So you don't actually have to sort anything into date order; it happens as you go. At the end of the financial year, you can hand the whole shebang to your tax professional for super-easy processing.

5   If you don't have a lot of receipts, or you can't be bothered sticking them all down, you can use a spike instead. If you use it every day, the spike takes care of the chronological order. At the end of each month, simply place receipts in an envelope and label accordingly. If you want to keep a tally on the front as you add the receipts to the envelope, make sure it's an A4 envelope.

Tips

✓   Maintain your system. The more frequently you sort your paperwork, the easier things will be at the end of the financial year. So try to file as you go. Make emptying your purse or wallet part of your routine. Record-keeping doesn't have to be a weekly chore; even spending a few hours once every month or so is helpful.

✓   Having a folder like this is a perfect opportunity to get your super-annuation better organised. If you have more than one account, take the time to combine them into one primary account. Super can be quickly depleted with administration fees, so save money by rolling multiple accounts into one. Of course, one account is a lot easier to keep track of too.

Filing: lever arch files

Lever arch files are my favourite way to file. They enable information to be stored easily on a shelf. Basic colour coding is easy. They are cheap to implement and the repetition is aesthetically pleasing.

It's a system that is easily added to, and best of all, there's not much paper that you can't punch a hole in. Even insurance booklets can be folded open and punched at the side (be careful not to chop any crucial information though).

While sheet protectors can be extremely useful (for example, to file away small scraps of paper, like receipts), be aware that they don't work well for bound or bulky documents and can require some maintenance – getting paper in and out can be a bit of a chore. Sometimes, if the documents are too heavy, the holes can rip. Worse, they can conceal the carefully labelled tabs that you've used to segment your information.

You will need

- 30 minutes or more
- a selection of lever arch files
- a pencil
- a hole puncher
- sheet protectors
- dividers

Method

1 Take the paper you need to keep and sort it into clear categories; for example, Visa, American Express, home loan, savings account, everyday account and so on.

2 Label a divider tab for each of the categories. Make sure you write on the tabs so they face the same way.

3 Starting with the last section, hole punch your categories and place dividers between them.

4 Do not overload the files: 75 per cent full is about right.

Tips

✓ Sheet protectors are perfect for housing things like:
- price lists
- sheet music
- frequently accessed information
- anything requiring a 'clean copy' for photocopying.

  The benefits of using sheet protectors are that:

- paper is protected from finger marks and grime
- it's nice and easy to swap around or replace large sections at any time.

  The drawback is that sheet protectors are not good for information that frequently changes or needs to be updated by hand.

✓ Avoid three- and four-ring binders unless you actually have a hole puncher to suit.

✓ Ring binders with pockets on the inside covers are fantastic for storing those extra-special or frequently used items.

✓ When archiving information, it is sometimes easier to archive the entire folder and start afresh for a new year.

Filing: suspension files and filing cabinets

Somewhere along the line, you've probably gleaned that a filing cabinet is the best way to store your documents. I don't agree. I call them 'graveyards for paper'. I don't use a filing cabinet and have never owned one. I have been in plenty of workplaces that have used them though, and it's true that they work for some people – and are sometimes beautifully maintained. Hooray! But many people struggle.

People who use filing cabinets tend to put things away never to look at them again. (This is truer of filing cabinets than of any other system.) It's easy to misfile or lose an important document between the suspension files. Creating tags and labels is cumbersome and labour-intensive – those little bits of paper can be tricky to fit into the plastic tab. If the brands of the suspension file and plastic tab aren't the same, they sometimes won't talk to each other. I find them frustrating and time-consuming. However, you might still prefer the filing-cabinet approach, or have a workplace that is full of them. If that's the case, let me show you how to use them best.

You will need

- 60 minutes or more
- a filing cabinet or plastic filing box
- suspension files
- manila folders
- plastic tabs
- paper inserts for plastic tabs
- a labelmaker or pen

Method

1 Start with an empty cabinet, or revise and rearrange existing files as you go. Decide on your principle categories: accounts/infrastructure, marketing, clients and so on.

2 For each file, use one suspension file containing one manila folder or more. For example, the staff file would have its own suspension file and might contain separate manila folders for employment contracts, leave application forms, time sheets and human resources information.

3 Create a tab insert for each file, and align the tabs of all the files within a single category (for example, left for accounts, right for administration).

4 Ensure the files are labelled consistently – for instance, you might have three insurance files in different places, but they should be labelled:

   - insurance – home
   - insurance – car
   - insurance – life.

Tips

✓ *Do not* overstuff individual files or the drawers. There must be plenty of room.

✓ When using paper inserts to label your suspending files, first roll the paper inserts gently (much like you might roll a cigarette) and you will find they slot right into the tab first time – a great timesaver.

✓ Regularly banish any 'must keep' files (archives) to a shed or long-term storage area away from day-to-day work areas. This frees up plenty of space, contributing to ease of movement, and means there is less to search through if you've 'lost' something.

✓ Use your filing cabinet as a clever home safe. Friends recently travelled overseas and were broken into while they were away. Luckily for them, they had used their lockable filing cabinet to store their camera equipment and other valuables. Everything they locked up was 'safe' when they returned home.

✓ Throw out any rusted, warped, torn or broken suspension files immediately. Replace them with new ones, preferably the kind with a small plastic critter on each end that will help them slide easily.

Filing: magazine holders

Magazine holders are perfect for storing chunky information like product catalogues, phone directories or even – gasp – magazines! I love using them as an alternative to lever arch files, and two magazine holders house my work in progress. Make sure you have solid ones though. Cardboard ones are a rip-off: they are not designed to take any weight or be handled regularly, so why waste your money?

You will need

- 10 minutes
- sturdy magazine holders (plastic or timber)
- information for filing

Method

1. Sort your information into main categories.
2. Use bulldog clips to group larger categories together. Use plastic letter files to house smaller chunks of information.
3. Label the front of your magazine holder, and keep hoarding to a minimum.

Tips

✓ Paint or cover your magazine holders if you want to colour code them.

✓ Be aware that they are very heavy when full.

✓ Magazine-culling tip: imagine moving house with them – they are weighty! If you're storing magazines, keep only the last 12 months; ditch the rest. You can recycle some magazines: kindergartens or sometimes doctors' surgeries will take them, but they should be recent copies and in excellent condition. Op shops tend not to want them unless they are high-end magazines (like fashion or decorating), and I've been told off for trying to donate magazines that I thought were pretty decent. So think hard – it's probably time for the recycling bin. Magazines: 'too bad, so sad, bye-bye'.

Filing: archiving

Archiving is an absolute must so that you can clear the decks for the more important tasks at hand. At least once a year, archive as much paper as possible. Whether you are managing household filing or business records, you should keep only current information on your desk or right at hand. Most of your archives will be financial documentation, which must be kept for 5 years from the date of claim.

You will need

- 30 minutes or more
- archive boxes
- a hole puncher
- some stiff sheets of A4 card
- some sturdy envelopes to house smaller items like cheque stubs or old receipts
- a texta
- some fasteners: large fold-back bulldog clips, Celco slide clips (metal) or some Avery Tubeclip file fasteners (plastic)
- a cover sheet (see page 105)

Method

1   Sort information into primary groups or categories. House any smaller or scrappier items (cheque stubs, receipts) in an envelope and seal. Sticky tape a cover sheet on top of the envelope and tick the appropriate category.

2   Take each category of paper, top with a cover sheet and punch holes in it. Slip it onto a Celco fastener or Avery Tubeclip. Alternatively, secure pages together with a bulldog clip. Back each bundle with stiff card – this makes handling easier, particularly if it's not a large bundle. Place a cover sheet on top and tick the appropriate category.

3   Place bundles and envelopes into an archive box while keeping a 'running sheet' of the contents. This will save you plenty of time when you're sniffing out a particular document.

4   When you're done, type up the list, or photocopy the original hand-written list. The copy can be stuck on the box. (Better still, make three copies – one for the top and two for the sides of the box – so you'll be able to stack the box and still always be able to read the contents.) If the box contains financial records, consider adding the date when the whole box can be destroyed. If the boxes are stored away from your work area, keep one copy of the list right at hand – in the front of your filing cabinet is ideal.

Tips

✔   Be careful when choosing cardboard archive boxes: they must be very strong. The generic ones are terrible! They don't take much weight, and sometimes the coloured ink from the printing on the boxes will rub off on your hands. If you are using cardboard ones, they must be double-walled and have a hinged lid. Plastic is also OK; just ensure the inside base is flat, with no hubs for wheel space.

✓ Store your archives in a space that is rarely used, such as the top of the stationery cupboard or on a shelf in the shed or storage area.

✓ Archiving is for anything that you *must* keep but that is not 'current': old tax returns, insurance claims that have passed, backup information or financial documentation (what accountants call the 'paper trail'). *Always* keep any property documentation or any contract with an original signature on it.

Cover sheet

Filing: photos

Who really makes time to put photos in albums? It seems like a bit of a chore. An easier approach is to use lidded boxes with index cards. Sorting them this way can be a good prelude to putting them in albums, or forget albums altogether.

Photos seem to gather in a box or drawer and breed. It takes a huge amount of time and energy to create order when you have a backlog. Most people have trouble managing their photos because they do one of two things:

- They ignore them and never organise them at all.
- They get sucked into the detail, the minutiae, feeling that every picture must be perfectly labelled and filed.

Don't rush the process or feel you have to have it completed yesterday. That will only cause you stress.

You will need
- 60 minutes or more
- your photos
- photo boxes and index cards

Method

1   Sort your images into a photo box — where the images are stored vertically and separated by index cards. The index cards hold information about the images. This will also allow you to make notes as you remember them — not under pressure! If you're a scrapbooker, it's a great way to organise your pages too.

2   Start with the 'easiest' photos — a box that you may get through faster — so that you will feel inspired to continue. These could be the photos with a recent history, those that are fresh in your mind and for which you can easily remember places, dates and names. I personally like to complete smaller tasks first so I can focus on the bigger things without feeling distracted. It also means you're able to cross more off the 'to do' list faster.

3   Consider the stories you want to tell with these pictures. Which are the pivotal moments? What images represent milestones? Which photos best represent the life of the person being depicted? These things should be considered when selecting images.

4   Editors — whether they are dealing with photographs, film, text, sound or art — never use all the 'raw' footage or pieces produced. They have a size or length in mind for the finished piece or exhibit. Not everything has to go in a box or album. Discard anything that is poor quality, badly damaged or duplicated.

Tips

✓   If you have access to a scanner, consider compiling a CD ROM of your finest and favourite images. You will always have a master and/or backup.

✓ Make sure you deal with any current photos *straightaway*. As soon as they're developed, whack them into albums while your memories are fresh.

✓ When you have your pictures developed (or when you download them if they're digital), immediately chuck out the images that are fuzzy, blurry, too dark, overexposed, badly framed or just plain dodgy.

✓ Double prints are only useful if you do something with them. Try scrapbooking, posting them to friends or relatives, or creating a collage on the wall. Don't hang on to them without purpose; they're double the work.

✓ Just because you shot it doesn't mean you should keep it.

Filing: memorabilia

Everyone has special bits and pieces, but rarely do they give them a special home. Leaving letters and mementos scattered all over the house is not the way to preserve them. Choose a container (a chest or trunk is perfect) and you'll have a dedicated space for your personal archives for life.

Your personal archives – or 'chest of treasures' – will contain things that are part of your history. They are objects like letters, documentation, personal effects, childhood mementos, keepsakes and so on. When properly stored, your special treasures can be handed on to future generations neatly.

During an organising session, a favourite client once unearthed something with great sentimental value when we were sorting through a storage space. Among the dusty golf clubs, hardware supplies and old audio cassettes, he found a small framed picture that had once hung on the wall of his bedroom. He fondly told me the story of the picture – a horse about to jump a river – and recollected that as a child he had spent many joyous hours lying in bed wondering if the horse would make it. That picture evoked wonderful memories of his time with his godfather. (As his parents were sometimes absent, he often stayed at his godfather's house, and that is where the picture had originally hung.) As he finished the story, he burst into tears. I confess that I got watery eyes too. After some discussion, we decided he should hang the picture somewhere where he could connect with it from day to day and honour those great memories.

This is a good example of what I call buried treasure. It really is the stuff that matters. Should you ever have to flee your home (or office), this is the stuff you want to grab – the irreplaceable stuff.

You will need

- 45 minutes or more
- a chest, trunk, large box, crate or deep drawer – as a general rule, one archive box (30.5 x 40 x 26 centimetres) per decade should provide more than ample space for your memories

Method

1 Sometimes it's easiest to make decisions about memorabilia once you have a rough chronology. You can then see where there's an excess or gap in your history. Your personal archives can contain all kinds of things. There are no rules about what to keep – your history is unique to you. *But only keep what is practical and really special.* Saving every thread from your past is neither wise nor practical. You don't want volume; you want significant items.

2 Think about the kinds of articles that might be selected by a curator if your life were to be displayed in an exhibition. Bear in mind that you don't always need to keep 'the best'. There is much value in collecting 'ordinary' items. A shopping list that your Nanna wrote can be a really interesting item, telling a great story about her habits and lifestyle.

3 Make sure the item is in good repair. Too dirty or tatty is not a good look! Clothing should first be laundered and pressed, and often that task is best left to the professionals. If you have a collectable or vintage piece, you will need specialist advice from an archivist, as it's often worse to launder these items. Place textiles between

layers of acid-free tissue paper. Then pack with silverfish and moth protection (health food stores have good products). Larger items like wedding dresses should be contained in their own boxes.

4   Use clear zip-lock bags to keep items separate and protected (but note that these are not 'archive safe'). Envelopes work well too, and they allow you to clearly label the contents of each bundle. Sorting items like this may make retrieval faster and aid visual clarity.

5   Ensure your box has a snug-fitting lid and is kept in a dry place away from extremes of temperature. Don't store your box directly on the floor, where damp can invade.

Decision making

- What should be kept that would best tell your story?
- What's unique to you and your life?
- What are the items you would bolt with if your house were on fire?
- Which items are most symbolic or interesting?
- Which items are of most significance to you?
- Which items are obviously most loved or in the best condition?
- What do you have an excess of? (Do you really want to keep all your school books?)
- Which items represent defining moments in your life?

Tips

✓ Some items that you might like to keep:
- school exercise books
- school reports
- diaries or journals
- commemorative items, medallions, certificates
- love letters
- your first drivers licence
- souvenir tickets, theatre, film or art programs
- clothing (christening gown, baby clothes, school uniform, wedding dress)
- sporting medals or ribbons
- locks of hair
- artefacts from family members
- selected photos and videos
- significant newspaper or magazine cuttings
- poetry or stories
- almost anything from your childhood
- your first-home purchase documentation
- receipt from purchasing your first car
- souvenirs from your first or a special overseas trip.

✓ Don't archive:
- medals, crockery, silverware, teddy bears, childhood toys and special photos – get them on display! Honour special things
- collections of any description. They're much better out where they can be seen, accessed and appreciated

- foodstuffs, including wine (unless it's suitable for cellaring). Consume it and be done with it! I've seen many old, crusty, mouldy wedding cakes too – it was a nice idea at the time, wasn't it?

✓ Allow a little room for future items to be added if you only have one container.

✓ Consult an expert regarding any unusual, valuable or precious items. Serious archiving is best left to the professionals.

✓ Zetta Florence (www.zettaflorence.com.au) has a massive range of boxes, folders and acid-free materials, and can put you in touch with specialist archivists for hands-on assistance.

✓ It's OK to have an interim home for memorabilia – a place where it can collect from week to week that's easily accessed. A drawer or shoe box is fine, but you might also consider using a tidy file for a variety of paper – where you can easily store financial paperwork, entertainment information and memorabilia all in the one spot. It can live here before you transfer the 'keeps' to a trunk or larger box.

Filing: recipes

You might have been clever enough to have hand-written all your favourite recipes onto index cards or into a book over the years. Even better, you might have had a system passed down from family members, so it's extra-special. A collection of hand-written and well-organised recipes is a charming and concise way to store plenty of family secrets.

But if you're anything like me, you'll be tearing recipes out of the paper or magazines, and you'll hanker after a speedy way to get them organised. This recipe for recipes is for you! It makes sharing, storing and retrieving a breeze. Cull the magazines and keep only what counts.

You will need

- 45 minutes or more
- all your loose recipes
- a display book
- scissors
- glue
- A4 paper

Method

1   Divide recipes into groups, bearing in mind that broader categories work best. You could keep it as basic as two categories (sweet and savoury). Keep it simple and choose fewer than six categories.

2   Cut and paste smaller recipes onto A4 pages to maximise space. Try to keep it to fewer than four recipes per page for visual clarity, and only use one side of the paper.

3   Slide your finished pages into your display book.

4   'A zip-out' book (such as the Marbig Kwik Zip A4 refillable display book) or a skinny lever arch file allows for super-easy rearranging and updating.

Tips

✓   Flag favourite recipes using Book Darts or 3M Post-it durable index tabs.

✓   A sturdy exercise book can work beautifully too; the only drawback is that the pages aren't interchangeable.

✓   Consider typing up and printing any hard-to-read recipes.

✓   Go digital and scan everything if you have a computer: you can simply fire up the computer and there's your recipe. This is great for sharing too.

✓   A conversion chart or any other commonly used information is best kept at the front of the book.

✓   Lose the recipes you were 'going to cook'. Seriously, you're not going to make them. Chuck them out. If that concept gives you the shivers, do what my friend Cath used to do with her partner: one night a week they took it in turns to test a new recipe. Use them or lose them.

Finishing: work in progress

Work in progress (WIP) is all the stuff that you're currently working on. It might be:

- information you've gathered on products and suppliers for house renovations
- marketing material for an upcoming advertising campaign
- a tax return
- an insurance claim
- upcoming travel, or a celebration or gathering that you're organising
- revision materials for an upcoming exam or test
- anything that you've put on hold for the moment but that is about to become active again (what I call a 'backburner'). Study materials that are put aside while you're on holidays are a good example of this.

WIP is best stored right at hand, usually on your desktop, and often in a magazine holder. This can be in what's often called a 'tickler file', which I think is a dumb term, so let's just call it a desktop file. Sometimes, depending on the urgency or importance of the tasks, I also call it a 'very important papers (VIP) file'.

You will need

- 30 minutes or more
- paperwork and resources for your WIP
- sheet protectors
- manila envelopes
- sturdy envelopes
- bulldog clips
- magazine holder (optional)

Method

1   Gather together any paperwork for individual projects and place it in front of you.

2   Sort your paperwork by project. House your projects in sheet protectors, document holders, manila files, sturdy envelopes, or simply use bulldog clips to keep pages together. (Choosing one type of storage will produce a nicer aesthetic.) If you have more than a dozen works in progress, see what can fall off your list. Your focus will be stronger if you're not spread too thin.

3   Any projects that contain three or fewer pages may be combined into a broader category. For example, a tax return and an insurance claim could both come under the one heading of 'financial' until the paperwork grows and each project warrants its own file.

4   Depending on the volume of paper, you can store your projects upright in a magazine holder.

Tips

✓ Never overcrowd your WIPs. Allowing room to move within the container will ensure quick and easy access every time.

✓ Keep it moving – everything in a WIP file should eventually pass to the bin or your more permanent filing system (for instance, a filing cabinet).

✓ A mini-WIP file fits perfectly in a Beautone Docu Manager, which allows information to be broken into subcategories. Examples of headings could be:

- *buying a house file*: properties to see; properties viewed; first home owners' rebate; house-hunting tips; finance
- *job-hunting file*: current applications; recruitment agencies; copies of resume; job-hunting tips; archive (positions that didn't happen)
- *entertainment file*: cinema; music; DVDs; books; shopping.

This type of file is perfect for housing information that is rapidly changing or needs instant access. The paper stays snug and the system is simple. House the fattest group of papers at the rear and more current towards the front.

Finishing: paying bills

Sorting a system for your bill paying has never been easier. This is pure low-maintenance!

You will need

- 5– 20 minutes
- your bills, paid, unpaid, receipts
- a highlighter
- a pen
- a stapler
- a rubbish or recycling bin
- a tidy file or filing trays (five drawers is ideal; three is the bare minimum)

Method

1 Gather all your financial documentation in one place. It doesn't matter where you put it, but it needs to have a *home*. Avoid the trap of having more than one home for your financial paperwork and you won't waste valuable time looking for it.

2 Label drawers:
- 'bills to pay' (top drawer)
- 'paid bills' (second drawer)
- 'house items' (third drawer), for items like your cheque book, stamps, envelopes and so on.

If you have more complex paperwork — for instance, if you run a small business — then the fourth and fifth drawers can house any accounting, budgeting or financial resources (even a calculator). My drawers are labelled 'to enter (MYOB)', 'to pay', 'bookkeeper', 'banking (cheque books, etc.)' and 'personal finances' (so that they are kept separate). Filing trays may be set up in a similar manner and work particularly well for higher volumes of paper.

3   Place all your paperwork in front of you. Staple together any loose pages to avoid wasting time matching them up later, and throw out the envelopes (in your rubbish or recycling bin). If a bill arrives with a reuseable envelope, paperclip it to the invoice ready for payment. Circle the total amount and the due date with a highlighter so that you're only visiting that information once. Mark in your diary or calendar when the bill is due.

4   Once you've done this to all your bills, place them back in the top tray. Either pay each bill on the due date when it appears in your diary *or* ignore bills for a week or two and pay multiple bills at once. Just about every bill you receive can be paid within a two-week period, unless it's already overdue (in which case you should pay it immediately).

5   If you've received a final notice, you should pay it immediately or telephone to make arrangements if you are unable to pay that very day. No one who's owed money likes being ignored. If you simply communicate and are reasonable, most people are satisfied with part payments.

6   When paying bills, keep accurate documentation. Once a bill has been paid, cross the front with a diagonal line, and make a note of the date, the method of payment and the amount paid. Marking the

invoice with a diagonal line is a visual tool: you know in a nanosecond that the bill's been paid. You know from across the room even! Now place the bill in the paid drawer. It can stay in the drawer until you have paid everything for that week and then be transferred another time to a filing cabinet, lever arch file or whatever filing system you use. The important thing is to know where the *current* bills are.

7   Following a routine will ensure success. Focus on the task once every week or so and your bills will always be taken care of. Open mail; enter data; pay bills; do filing. Easy. I like Mondays for 'accounts' simply because it's the start of the week. I'm not mad about doing bookkeeping, but I *love* having a routine because I know that it will get done – and when it will get done. I also allow enough time to plan for tax time, to see the bookkeeper and accountant, and to archive the paper trail.

Tips

✓ Investigate BPAY and internet banking. Some bills – like your rent, phone bill or insurance instalments – are best paid by direct debit. Speak with your financial institution if you're not sure how to go about it, or ask a friend in the know to take you through the process. It's easy!

✓ If your cash flow isn't great, prioritise your bills. Make a list of the payee and the amount, then rate them 1–10, bearing in mind the due dates.

✓ You can 'pay' bills before the due date – simply schedule an internet payment for the due date. If you pay bills by posting a cheque or money order, organise the payment in advance and simply hold on to the envelope until the due date. Write the date that it can be posted on the top right-hand corner in the spot where the stamp goes. The date will be covered when you post it. Easy, huh?

✓ It is important to look at your accounts once a week or once a fortnight. Block out time in your diary to attend to it. As a general guide, for a self-employed worker or a household with paper-generating finances like investments or self-managed super, you should allow about a day a fortnight. If you just have regular bills and there's one or two of you, you'll have very little financial record-keeping and could get away with an hour a fortnight (or, better still, half an hour per week). Don't skimp on the time you devote to this: attending to financial matters will save you money. An investment in time now means savings in your pocket later. No cut-off phone or late fees. No stressful moments!

Finishing: dealing with mail

If you don't know where to start with the pile of mail that collects at home or work and feel stressed every time you look at it, you're not alone. I recently discovered that a good friend has no routine for checking his mailbox. When I asked how often he checked the mailbox, he said, 'Don't ask!' Once a week? I suggested. 'Don't ask!' he cried. Part of the secret to managing paperwork is to open your mail regularly.

You will need
- 10 minutes
- unopened mail
- opened mail
- a rubbish or recycling bin
- your diary or calendar
- a pen
- a stapler

Method
1 Do it now! Dealing with the mail as soon as it comes in – or at the *very* least, later that day – is the ideal way to go. If you can do this, you are less likely to have an insurmountable stack.

2   Open it over the bin. Discard any junk mail or anything that's not immediately of interest – that's anything you are not definitely going to read, act on or file. Staple together any related paperwork; for example, two pages of a bill.

3   Handle each item once and be decisive. Avoid the 'deal with it later' pile and you'll never have to return to double handle. This is a great timesaver.

4   Cancel subscriptions to anything you don't make time or have no inclination to read (or don't really value). Apply the same rule to email. If you don't read it, you don't need it. Create a folder of the organisations or publications that you need to contact (by writing, emailing or calling) to be taken off their mailing lists. If you have more than two or three lists from which you want to be removed, it's a more efficient use of time to do these things as a 'job lot' rather than being distracted and taking time out from the task at hand.

5   Whether they are personal or work-related, keep invitations, event notices, study dates and appointment details all in one place, and make sure you put them in your diary as soon as you receive them.

Tip

✓   Much of the mail we receive is marketing, so be clear about what you might be shopping for *before* you open the mail.

   Dealing with paper as it arrives in your life is a crucial management strategy. It will ensure you don't end up with a fat office or study.

Finishing: pre-filing

Filing trays are often misused. 'In' and 'Out' mean nothing, 'To do' will end up too fat and 'Filing' often results as a tower of neglect. Trays are best used for what I call 'pre-filing', which will help you avoid unmanageable stacks of paper. It's a great way to keep an eye on the bigger picture.

You will need
- 30 minutes
- up to four filing trays
- unsorted paper for filing
- labels

Method
1   Head straight to your filing map of four categories (see page 88). Let's say your categories are marketing, clients, accounts and infrastructure. Simply set up a tray for each category and your filing is half done. I have a minimum of one filing afternoon a month, and I file in two stages. I have only one filing pile, but as it starts to grow, I do a very quick sort into the pre-filing piles. Breaking the filing down into separate chunks makes me feel less overwhelmed by the thought of doing it. I get a minor sense of achievement because something is going to run more efficiently as a result. (OK, I'm a bit in love with functionality. But I love form too!)

2 Your pre-filing can work in other ways too: simply stacking two trays on top of a filing cabinet can allow you to delineate between the drawers. It can halve the job – literally.

Tip

✓ Pre-filing gives you an important break from computer-based tasks, or from sitting at your desk. It's a good activity to stretch your legs and use different parts of your body and brain.

✓ Try not to have more than half a dozen trays unless you plan on using what's called a 'literature sorter'. These probably work well for hands-on creative types or for those who need to shuffle multiple projects. They are generally timber and can sit on a bench or desk and have between nine and 100 slots.

✓ Other uses for filing trays:
  - housing chunks of paper, like blank paper and letterhead
  - a home for paperwork to be processed; for example, job sheets that need to be invoiced, data entry for the computer
  - grouping like objects; for example, using the top tray for all your postage supplies.

Finishing: reading

Unless you're a voracious reader, I do not recommend keeping a pile of reading material that you're 'going to read'. People who say they are 'going to read' are generally not the kind of people who make time for reading. True reading material is 'active' (it's by your bed or on the lounge or in your bag); it's not in a pile gathering dust bunnies. Unless it is a book, like this lovely little critter, most of your reading matter will be pretty disposable.

You will need
- 5–20 minutes
- your stack of reading matter including magazines, newspapers, books and so on
- a highlighter
- some 3M Post-It durable index tabs or Book Darts

Method
1. First, separate your pile into:
   - newspapers and junk mail
   - books
   - print-outs
   - miscellaneous paperwork (forms to fill out, newsletters, journals and so on).

2 Reduce the rubbish. Don't tell yourself, 'I was going to read that'. You've got a busy life. If it had really mattered that much, you would have made the time to read it when it was first in front of you, not left it to languish in no man's land. Make sure you also dispose of any junk mail or obvious rubbish as you go.

  Throw out the newspapers unless they're today's. Don't read them again! Don't do anything more than give them the vaguest glance as they move to the recycling bin.

3 Put the books that you are reading next to the bed (if you read in bed). If there are more than three, then put the additional books back on the bookshelf, or return them to the library or the person you borrowed them from. Keep professional and reference books separate from fiction and fluff.

4 If you are a passionate reader, then create a space in your home or workplace dedicated solely to reading. If you have many books, consider grouping them by genre, author or topic. *Do not* overstuff your bookshelves. It's disrespectful to your books, and putting them away or retrieving them will become a stressful chore.

5 For any paperwork that requires action, see page 82.

6 Allocate one central home for any remaining material you can't part with just now: a very small selection of magazines that you are still browsing through or value *highly*, a cookery book you will be using within the week, or a professional journal or report that requires some focus and attention to properly digest. Also keep any irreplaceable items (original documents that you could not possibly get again).

7 Allocate time to read by adding reading to an already established routine. For example, read for twenty minutes each morning in the office over coffee or juice, or when there's a half-hour break between favourite television shows.

Tips

✓ Using a basket for your reading matter creates a lovely aesthetic, but it is not very practical – horizontal layers are hard to get to, and magazines will generally just gather dust. I suggest dealing with the content (read it, then chuck it) instead of storing it. You can always tear out the 'must-haves'.

✓ Magazines, newspapers and print-outs are highly disposable items – especially print-outs from the internet.

✓ The recycling bin is the best place for most of your reading matter. As a general guide, about 5–10 per cent of what you keep will possibly be read, and about 3 per cent is actually incredibly useful and irreplaceable.

✓ If you absolutely have to keep magazines, keep only the last twelve months' issues of no more than two or three titles.

✓ Any paperwork that is replaceable or time-sensitive should be thrown out. A good example of replaceable paperwork is a catalogue that you are not likely to purchase from, and an example of time-sensitive paperwork is the flyer for the fun run that is on next Sunday and for which you haven't trained. Be realistic.

Forwarding: outgoing

Sending thank-you notes, responding to invitations, returning questionnaires and remembering to get that book back to the library are all examples of items that need forwarding.

You will need

- 20 minutes or more
- a tray or shallow drawer
- any mail to which you need to respond
- anything needing copying before sending
- stamps, envelopes, paper and so on

Method

1   Sort your mail according to the type of response that's needed: surveys or forms to fill out; typed letters; quick hand-written cards.
2   Prioritise according to date sensitivity.
3   Draft any letters that require typing, checking or special care.
4   Have a routine to deal with correspondence.

Tips

✓ Keeping your postage and supplies in a central place will guarantee ease of retrieval and will also save time. When envelopes, stamps, address stickers and paper are all kept in the same place, the task becomes a pleasure, not a chore.

✓ A self-inking stamp or small stickers are a great way to save writing your address on the back of envelopes over and over.

✓ If you have an item to return to someone, or a purchase that needs exchanging, keep it right by the door so that you can grab it next time you're on your way out (instead of running late because you can't find it).

On the go

Life is busy. Our list of commitments, responsibilities and demands on our time seems to be never-ending. Being able to manage things well involves task-, project- and time-management skills. Don't worry if you aren't always on top of these things – it's not really possible to do everything you want or need to do all the time. You might not ever tick everything off your 'to do' list, but you can be better organised.

Using a notebook

Using a notebook is far more effective than making notes on scraps of paper or leaving sticky notes all over the place. Make sure you use only one book if possible. An A4 notebook is great, but A5 (half the size of A4) is even better because it is compact and can be thrown into a bag if need be.

You will need

- 15 minutes or more
- a notebook (A5 or A4)
- a pen or pencil
- a ruler
- sticky tape
- information for your notebook
- paperclips or bulldog clips

Method

1   Mark the cover of the book with today's date. When the book is full, add a 'finish' date. This makes archiving – and retrieval – very efficient.
2   Rule a line along the left-hand margin, and date entries as you add them. For example:

21.2.07	Phone sparky re down lights.
24.2.07	Speak with Richard re Wilson's Prom trip. Has he confirmed booking?
25.2.07	Email Julia about house for sale in Thornbury.

3   If you have lots of scraps of information on little bits of paper to transfer, consider simply sticking them all down with tape instead of transcribing them. Only transcribe existing notes if it's quick and easy.

4   When a task has been completed, cross it off with a highlighter or pen. When a whole page is completed, cross the entire page with a diagonal line so it's clear that page is done.

5   Use a large paperclip or small bulldog clip to separate the 'done' pages and to take you straight to the current pages.

Tips

✓ Date everything you add – otherwise you will forget or will have to rely on memory. Dates are most useful in determining chronology ('When did we speak?') and currency ('Oh, that price is from last year').

✓ A highlighter allows you to 'flag' important information for swift retrieval.

✓ Use both ends of the book. The front could be work-related; the back could be personal 'to do' items. Or the front could be used for daily tasks, while the back could be reserved for weekly, monthly or longer-term tasks and projects. You can either use the book normally front and back, or you can flip it vertically so that it always feels at though you are working from the front.

✓ A notebook that has perforated pages allows you to rip out pages and neatly file them elsewhere if you need to.

✓ Use only the right-hand pages of the book. This leaves the left-hand page free for updating notes or adding further information.

✓ A very small (ideally spiral-bound) notebook is a great tool for keeping frequently used information (such as login details for a website, or numbers like your ABN or membership numbers). My brother Luke calls this kind of notebook a 'grass catcher'. A grass catcher works best in your pocket or bag as a place to jot your thoughts, quick ideas and any phone numbers or shopping lists (including measurements for renovation materials). The idea is that your grass catcher is emptied regularly, just as it is when you mow your lawn. Much of what you collect is probably 'disposable', but anything requiring longer-term storage can be transferred to your phone book, diary, browser bookmarks or project file.

✓ Like a notebook, you can use the front and back of your grass catcher to divide information and tasks into two main categories.

✓ Keep a retractable pen together with your grass catcher for maximum efficiency.

Diary and calendar management

There is no doubt that there's a direct link between a lack of organisation and a lack of time management. The better you are at managing your time, the better organised you are likely to be.

You will need
- an hour or more
- your diary or calendar (only *one* of each)
- a pen or pencil

Method

1 Choose a diary that best suits your needs: everyone is different. Ring-binder diaries (such as Filofax or Poco diaries – see www.pocoprofile.com.au) allow flexibility and offer refills that enable you to customise your set-up. Book-style diaries work well for old-fashioned types like me. A calendar makes information-sharing easy – for instance, the whole family can check everyone's schedules at a glance

2 Plot any birthdays, anniversaries, holidays and significant dates when you start a fresh system.

3 For diaries, enter all bills to be paid and other important dates like birthdays at the very top of the page so that you are consistent. If information in your diary acts as a prompt for action – for instance,

if you invoice regularly based on client bookings or on employment time-keeping – tick the prompt when it's done so that you know it's been processed. It's a simple system, but often overlooked.

4   Check your diary or calendar at least once a day. Scan the coming days or weeks to check what's coming up. Planning equals organisation.

5   Frequently used numbers can be kept at the front of your diary: ABN, bank account numbers, membership numbers. *Never* store your personal identification numbers or passwords in the same place, no matter how 'coded' you think they are. It's a recipe for disaster. Use the yearly planner at the front to flag future events: tentative conference dates, travel plans, babies due or deadlines for projects. Having a bigger picture is part of being organised. It doesn't hurt to double up and note the dates within the diary too. Girls, use the yearly planner to circle the dates of your menstrual cycle so you always know the date of your last period. I also use the yearly planner at the front for regular tasks like car servicing, carpet cleaning and hairdressing so I can easily plan and budget the next time they're due.

Tips

✓   Kikki K's family planner ($24.99) makes kid-wrangling easy. There are very few products on the market that will truly help you get organised, but this product is very useful when used correctly.

✓   Archive old diaries and calendars for twelve months (personal) or five years (business).

✓ Any information that is regularly updated or added to – such as weight, staff availability, or worming or health care for pets – is best kept in your diary.

✓ Consider a financial year diary. This way, you can avoid feeling obliged to shop for a diary when the temperature hits 40 degrees Celsius, you're hung over and your belly is too full of prawns and cold ham sandwiches.

● Birthdays

● Keep a birthday calendar on the wall in a central location (one friend uses the back of the toilet door so that she has no option but to be reminded). I have a typed list that I alter by hand and update when it gets too messy. The date and year of birth sits under each monthly heading, and I transfer these dates into my diary every three months. I make sure I include a 'send present/card' ten days prior, so I'm not leaving it until the last minute. This is a particularly good technique when it comes to organising something for a friend or family member overseas.

● Use your mobile phone calendar to set a reminder for very important dates – those special dates that really shouldn't be forgotten.

Contact details

- Write in your address book in pencil: it allows for easy updates.
- Ideally, use a diary and phone book in one. Two books can be messy and cumbersome.
- First up, stop collecting all those business cards! You *really* don't need them. Have a decent cull. If they're important enough to keep, then take the time and put them in an index card system (but it had better be big, because I know you are going to collect more). I reckon we use 5 per cent of the cards we keep.
- If you can't bear to cull your contacts, then at least keep them all in the same place and try to throw out one old one when a new one arrives. A small, shallow drawer or box without a lid is ideal to house them.
- The other option is to add contacts to your computer: Microsoft Outlook allows you to keep all your names and addresses in a central place. It takes a little time to enter all the contacts, but once you're done, it's simply a matter of maintenance. Just make sure you back it up regularly (see page 65).

Pin boards

If you're a visual person, or you're the teensiest bit creative, or you simply like having things on show (to remind you), then let me share some of the best pin board organising secrets around. A pin board can quickly end up looking like you've started a paper recycling plant on the wall. Don't go there! The solution is to use only small things or items of a similar size. Also, don't layer the paper! Why has no one ever told you this before? Because it's one of the most closely guarded design secrets in the world. Stylists take it to their graves.

A pin board full of A4-sized paper will rapidly become swamped unless the sheets are carefully pinned side by side like at the local lawn bowls club. Use a display book instead. It's ideal for lots of printed information (particularly A4 size) or for information you need to refer to on a regular basis.

If you have a pin board space, consider its use. A pin board is best used for honouring memories, and for items such as favourite photos and small bits of information like business cards, favourite words clipped from the newspaper or a magazine, or a compact list of important numbers. These are ideal items because they're small and you can play around with how you display your lovely things. My pin board also has a printed list of dialling times for the United Kingdom so I can ring mates abroad without having to look the times up every time. Call me organised, but I even have a list titled 'summer' and one 'winter' so that I never have to get confused about daylight savings.

You will need

- 30 minutes or more
- a pin board
- pins
- stuff for your board
- a rubbish or recycling bin

Method

1 Remove everything from your pin board. Put all the pins in a small dish.
2 Sort into piles according to size: A4, A5, other little critters like business cards. Chuck the rubbish as you go (make friends with your rubbish bin).

3   Return selected items to the board. Start with the biggest pieces you have. Add smaller stuff in sections, grouping by colour, size or theme.

4   Small groupings work well; for example, a grouping of all your business cards. Allowing some 'white space' also works well.

5   Keep spare pins on the board, right where you'll use them next.

Tip

✓   Tiny boards (say 60 x 30 centimetres) should be avoided.

'To do' lists

I love a bit of list action. A written list provides direction and mental clarity. It's all part of having a plan. It also makes tomorrow easier (which is my primary motive for being organised – if I'm organised today, I'll have more free time to do nothing tomorrow).

Creating a list is only the first step. Actually *doing* the things on that list is the second step. In the film *Pieces of April*, Katie Holmes plays a young woman trying to get organised to cook her family turkey at Thanksgiving. Never having cooked a turkey before, she is slightly overwhelmed by the task at hand. She turns the oven on to pre-heat then sits at the kitchen table and writes 'To Do' at the top of a blank page. Underneath, she writes 'pre-heat oven' and puts a line through it. That's certainly one way to make a 'to do' list!

You will need
- 20 minutes
- a notebook or paper, or computer and word-processing software

Method
1 List action tasks one by one, estimating how long it will take as you go. Planning your time this way enables you to feel more in control and to use more small grabs of time in your day. Break down large tasks into smaller chunks and you won't feel so overwhelmed. You'd be surprised to find that most tasks take 15 minutes or less.

2   Be specific, and use detail. Let's say you want to go on holidays. Writing 'book holiday' isn't quite enough. A better list might look something like this:

- Put in a holiday request form at work   10
- Email Elana to confirm dates   5
- Collect passport renewal form from post office   10
- Look at flights to New York via Hawaii on the internet   20
- Google accommodation in NYC   20
- Check savings account balance   5
- Rough out a budget   20

Now you know it's 90 minutes' work, but the various tasks involved are much more easily digested and acted upon.

3   Cross off items as you complete them. Date any relevant information or simply date the top of each page. Note any specific dates on your calendar or in your diary.

Tip

✓   Keeping too many lists is overwhelming. Learn to let go of the stuff you are not likely to complete.

Shopping lists

A shopping list that is on a blackboard in the kitchen probably looks quite stylish in the magazines, but unless you are taking the blackboard to the shops, it's a list that will need transcribing to paper, which means you are doing the job twice. Simply sticking a pen and paper to the fridge is one of the simplest and most practical ways of keeping tabs on your shopping needs.

A smaller, more permanent shopping list should be housed in your wallet or purse, and should contain crucial details of infrequently purchased items like printer toner cartridges (list exact make and model), vacuum cleaner bags and any other purchases that we often get wrong. Many of these items are very expensive to purchase, and too often we buy the wrong ones because we rely on memory or chance.

You will need
- 20 minutes
- a pen and paper
- a magnetic hook or clip for fixing to the fridge

Method
1   Open the pantry door and check fridge for 'missing' items or popular, frequently used supplies.

2   Note items needed according to major categories:
   - dairy and frozen foods (milk, butter, yoghurt, tofu, ice cream, souvlaki, bread …)
   - household items (loo paper, paper towel, Windex, light globes …)
   - toiletries (deodorant, cotton buds, tissues …)
   - pet food (crunchy bits, kitty litter …)
   - fresh food (fruit and vegetables, fish, bread …)
   - errands (prescriptions, key cutting, newsagent, DVD return, dry-cleaning, hardware or any errand that will take you beyond the grocery store, like purchasing olives from the Greek deli). This part of your list is just as important, if not more important, than your shopping list. We often forget to do this kind of shopping, so keeping it as a separate heading is important. I use the top part of the paper for groceries, and the bottom part for errands.

      Grouping items this way means you can shop sequentially when at the supermarket, travelling with ease between one department and the next. You'll be the most efficient shopper there! No traipsing back and forth along the isles; you'll be in and out in the quickest possible time.

3   Remove your list from the fridge once a week to do your shopping. Having a routine will really help – for example, you might do it on Thursday night before gym, or on Saturday morning after breakfast out.

4   Any missed items can be transcribed to a fresh list for the following week.

Tips

✓ Don't shop without a list or when you're hungry. You will forget important stuff you really need and buy 'bad' foods you don't need because you're thinking about snacking. This can be very costly and stressful.

✓ Knowing your favourite meals and ingredients is incredibly useful. What are the foods you always love? My 'love list', for instance, would include red capsicum, fetta cheese and free-range eggs.

✓ Consider typing up and copying a list of frequently purchased and favourite items with check boxes next to them – you'll never go hungry again.

✓ If you can afford it, shop ahead. Buying in bulk is an obvious thing do to, but did you ever stop to wonder how long it would take to get through a sack of flour? Not ideal. Think more in terms of multiple packets of pasta or tinned foods. Super-size works a treat for washing powder and toilet paper.

Bag

Remember the old Glomesh magazine ads from the 1970s? Each ad featured a celebrity's handbag and the contents spilled across a table. I was always fascinated with what people kept in their bags. Of course, it was always very art directed – no leaking pens or old tissues. But I remember noting that the contents reflected distinct personalities. What does your bag say about you?

Don't worry if you don't use this recipe that often, but do use it at least once or twice a year. A bag that hasn't been sorted in a while holds hidden treasures – money, jewellery and mementos might magically appear!

You will need
- 15 minutes
- your bag and its contents
- a table or the floor
- a rubbish bin

Method
1 Empty the contents of your bag onto a flat surface, grouping like objects together (grooming, stationery, purse, phone and so on).
2 Chuck out any old tissues, old chewy, broken make-up, leaky, broken or excess pens and pencils, unimportant receipts, expired public transport tickets, spent reading material and old coinage.

3   Return to the bag your keys, wallet, glasses, packet of tissues, lip balm or lipstick, diary, phone, current reading material, pen, make-up bag, personal digital assistant, iPod and so on.

4   Consider segmenting items as you go. I like to keep a readily accessible compartment for train tickets, lip balm, phone and iPod, as these things are often in and out of my bag.

Tips

✓   Clear out your bag after several uses. For example, if you use a bag daily, it's a good idea to empty it completely once a week. (Sunday night is a good time to prepare for the coming week.)

✓   Only carry what you *have to*. Lose the excess baggage! Overloading your bag is unnecessary and can cause poor muscular skeletal health.

✓   If you are constantly swapping bags, make sure you clear them out thoroughly between swaps to avoid the 'Oh, damn, I didn't bring my sunglasses' scenario.

Car

Repeat after me: 'My car is not a dumping ground. My car is not a travelling rubbish bin. My car is not the spare room. My car is not an op shop. My car is a valuable and useful tool that I love and organise occasionally'.

You will need

- 15 minutes
- your car and all the stuff you've dumped in it
- a rubbish bin

Method

1 Start by removing all the obvious rubbish and recycling.
2 Put the street directory in the glove box or somewhere close to the driver.
3 Make a note of anything useful that you're running low on (fuel, fresh CDs, shopping bags, tissues, pen and paper) and replenish at the next opportunity.
4 Resolve to fix anything that needs attention. Don't spend years driving around with a broken lock on the driver's-side door or a busted radio because you 'haven't gotten around to it'. Your car is a tool. Tools should work, and they should be well maintained and easy to use (enjoyed even). Remember: that little bit of rust or that

slight puff of smoke from the exhaust is only going to get worse (and cost you more money). Get onto it straightaway.

5 Just because you have storage compartments doesn't mean you have to fill them. Don't use your car as a spare bedroom, where stuff lingers just because it doesn't have anywhere else to live.

Tips

✓ Here are some items that can be lifesavers and that are worth the space they take up:

- a first aid kit
- a fire-extinguisher
- a picnic rug or blanket
- maps
- bottled water (even if it's just for suburban driving)
- moist towelettes (for mucky hands when you have finished changing a tyre or for when you just need a quick hand clean)
- shopping bags.

I also keep spare disposable cutlery (I am always feeding myself on the go), and a coin purse full of change for the parking meter.

✓ Make it a priority to check your spare tyre and to check that the necessary tools are there for changing it. If you have never changed your tyre before, ask someone who knows how to give you a short lesson, or read the manual. Ask roadside assistance to show you next time they change it. Changing the tyre yourself is a simple job once you know how. If you've never done it before, it only requires minimal skill and a little practice. Many modern cars even have a visual marker to show you where to put the jack, so you can't really go wrong.

- ✓ Sunscreen and insect repellent are both great summer items to stash in the boot if room allows. Be warned that these products will deteriorate rapidly. I discovered this when I spent the day at what felt like the most fly-blown spot in Australia and I found that the prehistoric insect repellent I had in the glove box had turned to cottage cheese.
- ✓ When you turn on the engine, fill out your motor vehicle logbook while the engine warms (very good for your engine, and a very efficient way to run your car). Do it every time and you will rarely forget; it very quickly becomes habit. It takes less than a minute.
- ✓ If your job takes you on the road, make sure you have spare business cards and any other sensible backup items stored in a clear plastic sleeve or manila folder in the boot.
- ✓ Use the seats for passengers and the boot for storage.
- ✓ Clean your car now and then. You'll feel good about it and you'll be able to see out of the windows better.

Wallet or purse

Does your bum look big in this? A purse or wallet bulging with excess cards, receipts and scraps of paper makes finding what you need a (confusing) chore. Don't neglect something you use so often! Take a minute once a week or once a month to sort your wallet or purse.

You will need
- 10–30 minutes
- your purse or wallet
- a rubbish or recycling bin
- paperclips

Method
1 Empty the contents onto a flat surface.
2 Separate contents into categories:
   - business cards
   - receipts
   - coinage
   - notes
   - lists and scraps of paper
   - lottery tickets
   - gift vouchers
   - stamps

- photos
- discount vouchers
- obvious rubbish
- ATM receipts
- spare parts (such as small screws)
- other items (bandaids, condoms, sachets of cosmetic samples and so on)

3   Divide your cash:
- All your notes go back into one section of your wallet for happy spending. Keep this section *exclusively* for your notes to ensure fast, easy access. You will always be able to see exactly how much money you have. Don't mix your notes with receipts or scrappy bits of paper.

4   Return the cards you use all the time to your wallet. Segment them by keeping like items together: finance, health, and entertainment or discount cards.

5   Immediately copy any photos that are one of a kind: a picture of your mum when she was all 1940s glamour; a photo-booth snippet of you and your best friend Trace when you were both fresh-faced enough to wear bright-red lipstick and when her now twenty-something daughter was still an infant on her lap; the only copy of the first image of your newborn. If these photos are important enough to have in your wallet, they are important enough to be copied. Don't leave it to chance: wallets and purses routinely go missing over the years, and these things are irreplaceable. It makes me nervous! Scan or copy your treasured photos so that you have a backup of important memories.

Tips

✓ Five-dollar notes can be set aside in a safe place at home and used as savings. I know a woman who saved every single five-dollar note that came into her possession by placing it in a small box in a desk drawer. Within just a few months she had almost $1000 saved. It's a simple and easy technique to tuck away cash savings on a regular basis, and you don't really notice that money is 'missing'.

✓ All gold coins can be dealt with in a similar manner. I save all my gold coins in a long oblong container, and that is my pizza money for nights when I cannot be bothered cooking or funds for a movie or DVD when I'm not cashed up. This is the same box I keep my five-dollar notes in.

✓ Loose change in a foreign currency can be donated to UNICEF's Change for Good program (see www.sorted.net.au/links). Local currency is accepted too, so get organised and help kids in need.

✓ Blokes, make sure you have a receptacle to put your coinage in at the end of the day – a dish, wide-mouthed jar or small box works well. It can live on top of a chest of drawers, on a shelf or in the kitchen drawer.

✓ My brother and his former partner Kath had a 'money cat', a beautiful wrought-iron cat that stood holding a shallow circular dish. The dish housed all spare gold coins, ready for pizza! The cat used to sit right near the front door. It was a lovely sight, and oh-so-organised.

✓ As the old saying goes, 'Take care of the cents and the dollars will take care of themselves'. Abundance is a concept that we often struggle with, and sometimes we feel we do not have 'enough'. To have a cache of spare change – well organised and easily accessible – is one of the small pleasures in life. I know if my wallet is empty that my moneybox will, at the very least, feed me that day.

● Loyalty cards

Throw out any loyalty cards that you have never used or have used only once. So many are offered these days, and at no cost, so they are very easy to acquire. I do not keep the majority of loyalty cards for the simple reason that they can contribute to the minutiae that can drag me down. They also restrict my choices too much. If I have a card that offers me discounts at a particular retail outlet, it means I must take the time to plan to shop at that outlet, and to travel there, even if it is not the most convenient location.

Loyalty cards are of most benefit if you are *already* a regular customer. For example, I travel a lot, so my airline loyalty cards are worth their weight in gold. It would be foolish not to use them and they deserve a special place in my wallet; a loyalty card for a store where I once purchased two cushions does not. I am not likely to visit there again, nor will I be in the market for cushions for a long time. That card can go.

The worst loyalty cards are the ones that come with a directory listing multiple companies from which I can get a discount. Can you imagine? A whole book, which I must either carry around with me or take the time to read and *remember* so that I will know which companies offer products and services that are of relevance to me. It's way too hard.

Give me a choice of retailers and I will happily shop around and get the best deal. This is a great way to take advantage of the best prices and right products, and at a location that suits you. If you do the sums yourself, you will find that almost all loyalty programs require a very high spend for you to glean any benefit.

The stores that offer to keep my card are the best. Most video stores do not require you to use your card – better still, some offer a key tag, which can work very well.

Suitcase and travel

I write this from a spartan hotel room. I love the sense of being unencumbered when on the road. It's very liberating. But departing on a journey can often be a stressful time: deadlines to meet, arrangements to be made, work to complete, pet care and travel details to worry about. So allow plenty of time and plan ahead. And don't worry if you don't always get packing right. Practice makes perfect, and this recipe gives you all the easiest ways to tackle the task. A stress-free departure is possible.

You will need
- an hour or more
- your suitcase
- clothes, toiletries and so on
- any professional resources if it's a business trip

Method
1   Allow enough time to pack. Start doing your washing at least two days prior. Some of the stuff currently in the wash will be the stuff you wear all the time and the stuff you probably want to take with you. Allow enough time for the laundry to *dry*.
2   Gather all the possible clothes and toiletries you might take and lay them on the floor or bed.
3   Now halve them – you need an 'essential' half and a 'not essential' half.

4   Pack the essential half, ensuring your toothbrush and bedclothes (or change of clothes) are most accessible. Travelling is a dirty, tiring job, but someone's got to do it.

5   *Do not fill* your bag to capacity! If you are packed to capacity it will be hard work every time you take something in or out of your suitcase. Travel light and pack with a sense of order (segmenting smalls, toiletries, shoes and so on).

6   A suitcase or bag gives you a boundary (just like the walls of your home, the rooms within it and any storage like bookshelves or cupboards). To be organised, you must always have room for the future. You will probably make purchases while away, or you might be given a gift. Make sure there's ample room in that bag to bring it home!

Tips

✓ Buy the best quality bags you can afford. They will last you a lifetime.

✓ Identify your luggage with tags inside and out. A laminated business card is the best way to do this and costs just a dollar or two at a printer. It saves time hand-writing, and they'll last for ages.

✓ Include a plastic bag for dirty laundry.

✓ Save almost-empty toiletries and cosmetics (toothpaste, shampoo, hair styling products) and stash them in your suitcase ready to go next time you travel. Liquids are weighty, and the less you pack of these the better. Also, if they spill, at least it's not a full container. If there's only a tiny bit left while you're away, you can throw it out before returning home.

- ✓ If you don't have 'almost-empty' containers, consider sample-sized bottles of your favourite toiletries.
- ✓ Think versatile: shampoo can also be used in place of soap when laundering smaller items.
- ✓ Pack plenty of socks, T-shirts and underclothes; items like jeans and jumpers won't need laundering as often.
- ✓ Don't take 'just in case'; take '*I'll definitely wear it*'. Unless you are travelling for business, you will probably wake in the morning and pull on the jeans you wore yesterday (so a good supply of T-shirts is mandatory).
- ✓ Pack only versatile clothes. An outfit that requires a specific combination (for example, particular shoes for a particular frock) means you may end up with many items you only wear once. Choose your most versatile clothes, such as trousers that can be dressed up or down, and a cardigan or jacket that goes with everything.
- ✓ If it's hot where you're headed, you'll probably wear the most comfy pair of shorts you own most days. If it's an in-between season, you'll be wearing that cardigan or zip-up every day.
- ✓ When packing, button up shirts and 'shop fold' them (the way they are presented in a store). Wrinkles will show less this way. Better still, take non-iron items.
- ✓ Wrinkles in clothing are often caused by over-packing … make sure your bag is not bursting at the seams. Unpacking as soon as you arrive will minimise wrinkled garments.
- ✓ Over-packing is one of the biggest travel mistakes. Don't burden yourself. Lugging all that luggage is a killer on your back and stress levels. And it can be costly in terms of storing and transporting (particularly in the USA when you consider tipping). Travelling light might make a difference to your budget too: if you have too much

luggage, taking a taxi might be the only but most expensive option for transfers. A heavy bag could rule out walking or taking public transport, both of which are fantastic ways to get to know the place you are visiting.

✓ I was shocked when I weighed my backpack once while travelling around Europe: it was about 17 kilograms (*way* too much). Consider weighing your bag before you leave; it might be incentive enough to reduce the volume. My friend Lizzie would joke that she'd 'lost a few more grams' when she threw away scraps of paper or maps while on the road; it still makes me laugh.

✓ Make it your golden rule only ever to buy *flat* or small souvenirs, such as postcards to augment travel photos, a small painting or sketch, a sticker or fridge magnet. Better still, consider wearable items: I still wear rings from New York and London every day. Or consider a 'useful' purchase. My art deco sugar bowl is from Camden Markets in London. A brolly, bag, shoes or wallet are all fabulous and practical souvenirs. I love having things in my life that come with fond travel memories.

✓ If you are travelling overseas, you only need to take one voltage converter (provided one will cover all the countries you'll be visiting). The Korjo website has a complete adaptor guide (see www.korjo.com). Your laptop, mobile phone, camera battery and hair dryer can all be plugged into a powerboard, which is then plugged into the converter. How's that for a good idea?

✓ *Always* completely unpack after every journey. As you unpack, make a mental (or written) note about what you really used and what didn't leave your bag. You might be surprised at the results.

✓ Book your flights in plenty of time, unlike the woman I know who promised to pay for her elderly father's flight from Melbourne to Brisbane one Christmas. By the time she got around to booking the fare, the only return flight that was left cost her nearly $1000. Ouch!

✓ Keep a copy of your itinerary in your baggage. It also pays to email it to a browser-based address (such as Gmail or Hotmail) as you can generally get to the internet wherever you are. If you are travelling alone or to remote areas, make sure you leave a copy of your itinerary with someone at home too.

✓ Repair luggage promptly or wipe off any spills or dirt as soon as they appear. Neglect can often result in having to spend more hard-earned cash.

✓ If you are travelling with any equipment that requires spare batteries, it can be difficult to remember which batteries are fresh and which are spent. An easy way to flag the fresh batteries is to wind a rubber band around them to provide an instant visual marker.

Keys

How many keys are on your key ring? Do an audit and you might be shocked by how few you actually recognise and use regularly. Many key rings are burdened by excess keys (their locks unknown), key tags and key rings. They will add excess weight and bulk to your pocket or bag and only slow you up when you least need it. Not all key rings are fat, but check yours to make sure it's as lean as it can be.

You will need
- 20 minutes
- your keys
- a zip-lock bag or small jar
- a rubbish bin

Method
1   Remove any keys that are not immediately identifiable (this could be as many as 80 per cent). Store your excess keys in a dated zip-lock bag or jar labelled 'just in case' and place in a shallow drawer (see page 175). Dating the bag means that if you don't find the locks for those keys within the next year, you can fairly safely get rid of them. Most of us are not brave enough to heave keys straight into the bin, so this gives you a safe buffer zone.

2   Flag any 'very important' keys. These are your priority keys: house, office, car or post-box keys — any keys that are normally used daily. They should be visually easy to recognise. Identify them by using slip-on coloured rubber edges, by having coloured aluminium keys cut or by simply being mindful of their location on the main ring. Since most car keys are larger and easily identified, placing your house or office key right next to your car key will also make it easy to find. Sometimes using one extra ring will provide a visual clue that the key attached is a very important one.

3   Rearrange the order of your keys to suit their most regular use.

4   Remove any extra key rings or excess tags for visual clarity.

5   Regularly assess your key ring. You'll be surprised to see how many random keys end up there.

Tips

✓   Dabs of coloured nail polish will help you to match your keys to the right locks when there are multiple locks on the same door. Dab both the lock and the key and you will never have to faff about. This will also help anyone to whom you need to loan your keys. Visual clues mean less confusion.

✓   Spare keys from friends *must* be clearly labelled to avoid confusion in an emergency. They are best stored in a drawer (see page 175).

✓   As boring as it sounds, there's great value in routine. Store your keys in the same place: on the hall dresser, on a hook near the door, on top of the kitchen bench, in the door or in your bag. If you are consistent and use the same location, you will find them first time, every time, and you won't run late because you lost your keys.

- ✓ Consider registering your keys with a credit card protection company (credit card sentinel). Take advantage of any car dealership or gymnasium that offers you a numbered key tag and a free key-return service should your keys be handed in.
- ✓ *Never* record your car registration number or address on your key tag as it could lead to disastrous loss. If you must label keys with a tag, include a post office box or 'care of' address for return.
- ✓ Cull your key ring whenever you move house or office.
- ✓ If you jog or walk regularly, cut a spare house key and use a safety pin to pin the key to your cap, the hem of your shirt or within a pocket. This enables you to be 'jiggle-free', and you won't lose the whole set if out and about. My morning walk once took twice as long as it should have: my keys jumped out of my pocket and I didn't discover the loss until I was almost home. I was forced to retrace my steps (wondering the whole way what I might do if they were all lost). However, I was able to take comfort from the knowledge that I had given my mate John spare house and car keys as a backup. Getting inside my house to get my phone to call John might have been the second hurdle though. Make sure your spares are with a friend who is local, generally about the place (doesn't travel a lot or doesn't work very long hours miles from your place) and preferably whose number you know off by heart.

Living

I'll be frank. You're allowed to have a junk drawer. You're allowed to have some signs of life in your living space. Isn't that a relief? The following recipes will help you navigate many problem areas of the home and will take your organising to a higher level.

Living space

Are you trying to keep up with the Joneses? Aiming for a beautiful, 'perfect' home might not equate to being happy or fulfilled. Material objects are no substitute for human contact or intimacy or companionship.

My philosophy is that you can keep up with the Joneses all you like, but make sure you're keeping the balance. 'Stuff' won't make you happy, fill a void or keep you company. The 'richest' homes are those filled with life, love, character and, most importantly, signs of life.

A living space is for living, so don't slave away trying to make it look like a sterile magazine home. Signs of life give character and interest – a little like the creases on our faces! (Just be mindful that your home doesn't look like Keith Richards though.)

Keep flat surfaces clear. In every room of your home or office, you need flat surfaces to work: in the kitchen to prepare food, in the office to deal with paperwork, in the lounge room to read the broadsheet or play cards. Flat surfaces are not for storing!

The most valuable real estate is from eye level to waist level. This is where you should store your most commonly used items and, if you can, even leave some space for transit items. For instance, unopened mail could be left on the bookshelf, and the hall table could be used for items that need to be returned or to leave the house (such as dry-cleaning).

You will need

- an hour or more
- your living space and all that is in it (furniture and contents)
- rubbish and recycling bins
- an empty cardboard carton for op shop items

Method

1. Check the configuration of your furniture to ensure it suits your use of the room. Your set-up should allow for easy:
   - *traffic flow* – paths through doorways, access to windows
   - *air flow* – heating or cooling.
2. Living and moving in your living spaces should be easy. If it's not, rearrange or lose any pieces of furniture that are not absolutely necessary.
3. Put away anything that already has a home. If it doesn't have a home, create one. Do try to use your living spaces for living and relaxing rather than as a dumping ground. Put away regularly – at least once a week if you don't do it as you go.
4. Repair or discard anything that is broken – appliances, equipment or furniture.
5. Clear all surfaces and make sure that your storage – whatever it is – is not 100 per cent full or overflowing. Put unnecessary items in a box to go to the op shop.

Tips

✓ One of the tricks is to work with your existing habits. If you always kick off your shoes as soon as you're in the door, provide storage right by the door or at least have a big coffee table so that they can slide underneath.

- ✓ If you iron in front of the television, stash your ironing board in the hall cupboard right nearby. (Who irons in the laundry?) If you use the coffee table as a workbench for processing paperwork, allow a place for trays close at hand – a discreet spot on the shelves nearby is perfect.
- ✓ If you have too many ornamental items (pretty rather than practical) and you can't bear to part with them all, rotate items by packing away half for a few months at a time, or change them over with the seasons.
- ✓ Think laterally. That little-used dinner party platter or fruit bowl could actually be used as a dumping ground for keys and the junk that collects daily on flat surfaces. In a matter of seconds, you've turned something hardly used into something used all the time.
- ✓ Open the curtains or blinds from time to time. Clean the windows and vacuum the fly screen. Dust the horizontal surfaces. Cleaning is not organising, but it does reflect your love and care of your space.

Kitchen and pantry

Shelf split

It doesn't matter whether you are single and live alone, a busy parent in a house of five, a businessperson travelling and working long hours in your job, a young student or a retiree: the kitchen is the heart of the home. When at home, most of us spend as much as 80 per cent of our waking hours in this space, so make sure you have it sorted.

Run your kitchen like a commercially run kitchen. Commercial kitchens have to operate efficiently, so why not apply this concept to your home? A commercial kitchen is always well stocked, and putting things away is as important as planning ahead. Storage spaces are not overburdened with too much stuff, surfaces are for working, and floors are cleaned regularly. You'd be amazed what a massive difference can be made by giving these areas a little more attention.

Steal the chefs' trick and prepare some food as soon as you've done the grocery shopping; for example, wash your lettuce and wrap it in a damp tea towel, then store it in a plastic bag in the refrigerator to keep it super-fresh.

You will need

- an hour or more
- your kitchen and all that is in it (appliances, food and other contents)
- rubbish and recycling bins
- an empty cardboard carton for op shop items

Method

1 Check the configuration of your furniture and equipment to make sure it suits your use of the room. Make sure you allowing for easy:
   - *traffic flow* – paths through doorways, access to windows
   - *air flow* – heating, cooling and exhaust
   - *access* – to the most frequently used places like the fridge, the cupboard with the drinking glasses and so on.
2 Working in your kitchen should be easy. If it's not, rearrange or lose any pieces of furniture or equipment that are not absolutely necessary.

3   Put away anything that already has a home. If it doesn't have a home, create one. Put away regularly – at least once a day if you don't do it as you go.
4   Repair or discard anything that is broken – appliances, equipment or furniture. Clear all surfaces and make sure your storage spaces are not 100 per cent full or overflowing. Put unnecessary items in the op shop box.

Tips

✓   Empty the freezer at least once a year. In December, I keep an eye on the freezer contents and don't add to it. By the time January rolls around, I pick the hottest day I can to open the freezer and let it completely defrost (making snowballs is great fun for the kids). If you don't empty the freezer periodically, you will forget how old some of the contents are and end up with a lot of 'dead wood' (the stuff right at the bottom and underneath that will never be eaten). It's a great summer chill-out task.

✓   Chefs always lay out all the ingredients they need before starting to cook. This simple technique allows you to see if there's anything missing, so you don't get halfway through making a laksa only to discover you don't have any coconut milk. Be prepared and gather all the tools and equipment required too.

✓   A highly organised cook might also have a sink of hot soapy water ready when cooking starts so that dirty implements can be washed (or at the very least, soaked) on the go. It's a great feeling to finish eating and know there's just your plate and cutlery to wash up.

✓   Avoid using round containers within a cupboard or fridge: they waste valuable space. Stick with square or oblong – and stackable is even better. Decor's Tellfresh range is great – perfect for everything from spices to first aid items.

- ✓ Anything consumed daily should be purchased in bulk: bread, long-life milk, pet food and so on. Shopping in bulk means greater savings, and greater efficiency too as you won't always be dashing down to the shop at the last minute.

- ✓ Half-filled bottes of frozen water are terrific topped up with tap or chilled water for when you're out and about in summer. Freeze on an angle so that as the ice melts, it cools all the water.

- ✓ If you're tight on freezer space or only have one ice cube tray, make batches of ice cubes and empty them into a plastic container. It's more efficient than fumbling with the tray (particularly if you are serving a guest) and you never run out of ice by planning ahead like this. Don't keep empty ice cube trays in the cupboard. Use them or lose them. A rubber ice cube tray is the easiest kind to pop the cubes out of.

- ✓ Squeeze lemons when they're in season to make lemon ice cubes, and then empty them into a plastic container when set so that you can re-use the tray. Simply defrost the cubes whenever you need fresh lemon juice.

- ✓ Save faffing about by storing items where they are used. A good example of this is storing vases right under the sink because that's where you'll fill them before adding the flowers. Lie them down if you don't have a tall enough space. If they're round, place an old towel underneath to stop them rolling. Store shopping bags in the car. Just think about the object and where it will be used.

- ✓ A bead stacker (available from haberdashery stores) is perfect for any bits and bobs like screws, hooks, spare parts or other small items you need to store. They come in two sizes. Tip: don't over-tighten as the plastic thread won't stand up to it.

- ✓ A magnetic knife strip is ideal for frequently used kitchen tools: tongs, knives and scissors. It's great if you're a visual person and like to see where things live.
- ✓ When making salad or chopping onion and garlic for meals, I always double the quantity and store half for the next day's meal preparation.
- ✓ When cooking, make twice the quantity. A pot of soup can be dinner one night, and single portions can be frozen for a quick snack or meal when time is tight. Better still, it can become lunch for work or school the next day, saving you a bundle in cash. I *love* home-cooked meals and snacks that are nutritious and ready to go.
- ✓ The Tupperware jumble can be avoided by using a deep drawer instead of a cupboard. It's easier to see what you've got and lay your hands on it quickly. Taking lids off means more space; keeping lids on means that no matching up will be necessary. Do what suits you.
- ✓ Dedicate a wide-mouthed jar or screw-top plastic container to store a half-used onion. It will keep your cut onion or garlic fresh, and also keep the stink out of the rest of the fridge.
- ✓ Freeze whole chillies so you'll always have them on hand. Simply run under hot water to defrost, or do what I do: carefully chop them while they're still frozen before adding them to the mix.
- ✓ Add something to your existing routine: in the morning while the kettle boils, take five minutes to put away the clean dishes on the rack or in the dishwasher from dinner the night before.
- ✓ Use shelf splits to double your space. Almost all kitchen cupboards are too deep and too high. Width is rarely a problem. Adding a half-shelf will give you valuable storage space, and being able to see

what you've got means you won't double-buy items you already have. You'll also save time looking for things.

✓ A well-stocked pantry should contain plenty of basics that can contribute to meals, such as tinned tomatoes for pasta sauce; tinned tuna for salad (or as a backup when you've forgotten to buy more cat food); coconut milk for curries; rices; cous cous (great in salads); dry biscuits; nuts; dried fruit; dried peas; and what I call 'emergency milk' (little jiggers of UHT milk for tea and coffee or 1-litre cartons for cereal and cooking). Be like a scout and 'be prepared'!

✓ Mugs and cups are best stored in drawers. Placing them upside down will prevent dirt or spills from getting into them, and you'll save time cleaning.

✓ A paper towel on the glass platter in the microwave provides a quick and easy way to clean up any spills without washing the plate.

Drawers: coffee table, kitchen and hall

Yes! Yes! Yes! You are allowed (and encouraged) to have a junk drawer. A junk drawer, no matter how junky, means you keep all kinds of little useful things in one place, and you know exactly where they are, which is pretty efficient. Your junk drawer can house all kinds of seriously useful ephemera, like batteries, bandaids, rubber bands, pens, tape, Blu Tack, takeaway menus, scissors, string, random hardware, a torch, loose change, spare specs, train timetables, chewing gum, spare keys and all the flotsam and jetsam that could otherwise mess up a bench top or drift aimlessly around a handbag, glove box or desktop. Even if there's non-useful stuff in a junk drawer, it doesn't really matter; it has a home. And it doesn't have to be particularly neat unless you are struggling to find things. The drawer closest to the front door is great for storing smaller items that need to be returned to their owner (such as a borrowed book or DVD).

You will need

- 20 minutes or more
- all the contents of your junk drawer
- rubbish and recycling bins
- an empty cardboard carton for op shop items

Method

1   Empty the contents of the drawer onto a flat surface. Sort and cull the contents. Make friends with your rubbish bin.

2   Segment into major categories, such as stationery, tools, things that leave the house (like sunglasses) and frequently used items.

3   Store any fiddly things or loose items in containers for better access – empty takeaway containers are perfect.

Tips

✓   Takeaway menus are best stored in a DL plastic envelope or in a plastic display folder with sleeves. At the very least, a bulldog clip can be used to keep them together.

✓   The best drawers are shallow and wide. Using a shallow drawer avoids creating horizontal 'layers' of stuff.

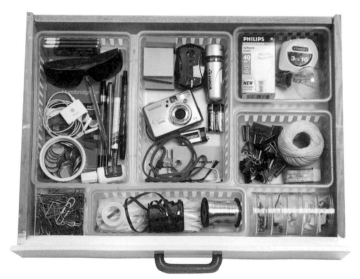

Utility spaces

A utility space can be the laundry, a store room, the shed or any dedicated storage space such as a hall cupboard.

You will need

- an hour or more
- your utility space and all that is in it
- rubbish and recycling bins
- an empty cardboard carton for op shop items

Method

1   Hang it up. Use the walls or the backs of doors to hang brooms, tools, vacuum-cleaner hoses, garden tools, the iron or anything that is light, bulky (a fan) or flat (the ironing board). Anything with a handle can be hung; a 'handle' can also be created by using a cable tie. Use your common sense: if it's heavy to lift, you will need serious hooks installed by someone who knows what they're doing.

2   Avoid placing hooks at eye level – both adults' *and* children's eye level.

3   Aim to reduce the contents of your storage space by at least 30 per cent.

4 Throw out any empty boxes that were packaging for a purchase. Unless you are planning to be a second-hand dealer or are moving house in the very near future, there is no reason to keep these (particularly if you are only keeping them 'just in case'). The exceptions to the rule are the box your computer came in, your camera box or the box for any high-end brand purchases (such as the box your Tiffany's jewellery or Rolex came in) as these will add to the item's resale value. Empty boxes take up a seriously foolish amount of space, so if you absolutely must keep them, flatten them out first and store them behind a freestanding cupboard or in a similar space.

Kids' spaces

In all my years of consulting (and nannying), space has never been an issue in kids' rooms. The volume of stuff is the problem. Toys, toys and more toys. Stuff everywhere. There are too many clothes, too many toys, too much furniture but rarely enough books. A favourite client, Anita, doesn't have this problem. Her toddler daughter, Bronte, has store-bought toys but is perfectly happy and stimulated playing with an old tissue box and a half-flattened balloon. Impressive! Obviously, not all kids are going to be easy to please, but ask yourself this: are the contents of your child's room more an indication of your attitude to stuff than a true reflection of your child's need for it?

Allowing your kids to have too much stuff is not setting a good example, and it creates many hours of maintenance for you (picking up and putting away). One client had toys in literally every room of the house, and they occupied more room than the adults had to entertain them. There was no limit on how many resources and materials their two very young girls had. With too much stuff, creativity is not enhanced; it's stifled. Children don't need every conceivable craft supply, as this client had arranged; they need to use their brains and to *discover* their own supplies. What's lying around the house that we can make into something: leaves from the garden? a paper plate? some old magazines and some paste? Whether you're a littlie or a grown-up, creativity is often best served by just a blank canvas and a little inspiration, either from your imagination or your environment. Taking a closer look at nature, for example, can be a good place to start.

I am not a parent, but I have worked as a full-time, live-in nanny, so I do know intimately what it's like. My organising skills were greatly appreciated in the family. I planned ahead, ran on time and generally kept the kids' rooms and belongings in reasonable order. I was never a slave to tidiness though: kids need to feel that they can make a mess and can live and play and create without getting into trouble.

You will need

- an hour or more
- your kids' space and all that is in it
- rubbish and recycling bins
- an empty cardboard carton for op shop items

Method

1   Hang it up. Use the walls or the backs of doors (including wardrobe doors) to hang swimming and ballet bags, school bags, raincoats, hats and sporting gear. Ideally this stuff should live as close to the front door as possible. Kids tend to use the 'floordrobe' a lot, so providing hooks will help them store their things with minimum fuss. Avoid placing hooks at eye level – both adults' *and* children's eye level.

2   Empty wardrobes and drawers, and sort the contents into the following three categories:
    - stay
    - go (for the op shop or second-hand dealer)
    - rubbish and recycling.
    Aim to reduce the contents by at least 30 per cent.

3   You are not allowed to have a 'not sure' pile, as this is simply deferring the decision and creating more work for later.

4   Pack up any clothing that is out of season or that is too small for your kids. Store and label according to size (for instance 'Size 6 – boys winter').

Tips

✓   The trick is to teach your kids how to maintain their space. As soon as children can walk, they can be taught to organise their space. A good technique is to say, 'Can you tidy up for me? Here, I'll help you'.

✓   Toys are best rotated: 80 per cent in rotation; 20 per cent packed away in a cardboard box in a storage area. This will enable you to introduce fresh toys from time to time to suit kids' ages, skill levels and attention spans. The introduction of fresh toys will keep your kids better stimulated. If your kids are under five, they are unlikely to remember everything they've got, as every day is full of new experiences.

✓   'Dump bins' or baskets are the easiest form of storage for kids to maintain. Avoid using lids, which are cumbersome, and make sure that they can easily get to the storage you have provided for them.

✓   A small set of wall-mounted shelves is best for any 'precious' bits and pieces.

✓   In your living area, allocate a basket or box for each child. Stray socks, toys, school work and so on can easily be placed in the basket or box, and then the whole container can be taken to the child's bedroom for a quick, timesaving tidy up.

✓   Organise a 'tidy-up' day with all your kids and have them get in on the act. Sort puzzles and put them back into their rightful places; put away any clothes; clean out under the bed; and throw away any broken or incomplete toys. Sort any craft supplies and throw out any textas that are dead. A great game is 'guess how many textas will go into the bin'.

✓ Teach them to look after their own things. This is an important life skill. Having too much stuff means they are likely to be careless with their belongings and not respect other people's things. Teach them to take care of what they're lucky enough to have.

✓ Kids thrive on routine because it means they know what to expect. Get them to empty their own rubbish bins, make their beds, put clothes in the laundry basket and keep track of their library books. If they are still young, help them with these tasks until they are old enough to do it on their own; the routine will be familiar to them by then.

✓ Make sure you get your kids to help you tidy up. Don't be a slave to fetching or picking up after them. A simple routine is to ask them once a week to pick everything up off the floor so that you can vacuum.

✓ Don't be a slave to the minutiae! Kids' lives and bedrooms seem to be breeding grounds for 'little things': little plastic toys, parts of games, texta lids, miniscule dolls' clothes, broken beads and tiny decorative things from heaven knows what. Have an ice-cream container for these things – a kind of sick bay for the lost and broken. Empty it periodically, but in the meantime, your poppet will know where to find her fairy princess's lost shoe.

✓ Don't ever try to sort your kids' stuff into rigid, specific categories unless they are more organised than you are. Broad categories like animals, Lego, dress-ups, soft toys and books are sufficient. Providing too many places to put things away will confuse them and make maintenance a boring, tedious chore (which is what we'd think if we were told to organise like that).

✓ Allow them a say in how their room looks, as this is one way they can express their personality, and creative expression is an important part of developing a sense of self.

✓ Encourage children to keep a small amount of memorabilia, but place a limit on how many pieces of artwork are kept. Photograph or scan the best pieces if you don't wish to keep the originals.

✓ Once they hit their teens, I'd close the door. Let them live in a mess. Who cares? You don't have to sleep there!

Gifts

Have a small cache of gifts ready to go for the never-ending round of birthday parties. This way, you will always have a present on hand. One of the best gift ideas is movie tickets – everyone loves going to the pictures. Movie vouchers are also a great adult gift, and the tickets are easily stored with your household paperwork or in the top drawer of your desk at work. Don't hoard generic gifts such as perfumed talcum power, body wash and little candles or picture frames. A gift with no thought is no gift at all; it's landfill. If you really care about someone, take the time to shop for something specific, but bear in mind that gift buying is a highly specialised art, regardless of how well you know someone. Sometimes it's best to ask the person what they'd *really* like. Or, at the very least, give them consumables like a meal out, a course, a balloon ride, or a membership or subscription to something they're passionate about.

Cosmetics

Cosmetics and toiletries often come in fiddly little containers that seem to breed the minute you pop them in your bathroom. And it's sometimes difficult to draw the line at how much is enough, particularly when random bath salts and body scrubs appear at Christmas.

A dear friend once had to clear out her bathroom before house renovations. I gave her a hand: everything she discarded from the bathroom, I placed into a large cardboard box. We filled it. As an experiment, I took all the moisturisers and cleansers home and used them. They lasted me just over a year! It gives you an idea of the volume of stuff we hang on to that we don't really need.

Women (and, increasingly, men) are under constant pressure to try the latest, shiniest, newest and most improved beauty supplies and toiletries. Let's be honest: you are better off spending more money on fewer products. That's what quality and economy are about.

You will need

- 30 minutes or more
- your cosmetics
- rubbish and recycling bins

Method

1   Sort your cosmetics into categories: hair, face, eyes, lips, nails and body work well.

2   Throw out anything that is not versatile, loved to bits or your first choice.

3   Shallow shelving or shallow drawers are generally the best storage. Avoid deep drawers.

4   Hang your hair dryer on a hook if you use it daily.

5   Make sure you use your most valuable bathroom real estate to store your most frequently used items.

Tips

✓   Recycle your unused cosmetics by passing them on to friends. It's better to pass it on than to leave it unused in your space.

✓   Discard any cosmetic that is damaged or old. A crumbly eye shadow isn't any fun to use or apply, nor is a gluggy nail polish.

✓   Look for versatile products: a moisturiser that contains a sunscreen, a lip balm that also works on burns or scratches (such as Lucas' Papaw Ointment) and so on.

Accessories

Jewellery is minutiae and a job best attended to when you have the rest of your space in order. There's no point in having beautifully ordered accessories when you can't find the car keys or the last phone bill. If you have a lot of jewellery (costume or the real thing), consider purchasing some plastic moulded jewellery trays from a wholesaler instead of using a jewellery box. They are velvet-lined and stackable, and can be placed inside a drawer or along a shelf that's below eye level. They come in different configurations suitable for earrings, necklaces, brooches and so on.

You will need
- 30 minutes or more
- your accessories
- a rubbish bin

Method

1   Sort your accessories into categories that work well for you. For jewellery, daily, costume and family might be good categories. Or you might sort them by colour blocking them, which always has a great visual impact.

2   Throw out anything that is never worn or that is not reasonably versatile. (Your versatile accessories are the ones that you always take away with you when you travel.)

3 Shallow shelving or shallow drawers are generally the best storage. Avoid deep drawers. Line the drawers with felt to prevent your jewellery from sliding and scratching.

4 Make sure that your most frequently used items are easy to get at and that your storage allows for more to be added to your collection.

5 Consider security: if your jewellery is valuable or highly sentimental, store it somewhere out of the way and lockable like your filing cabinet. You'll need to be consistent with putting it away.

6 Make a point of mending or remodelling anything that is not currently in use.

Tips

✓ Sunglasses, belts, ties and bags are all best stored on hooks or racks.

✓ Using the back of the wardrobe door is a great way to use a forgotten space and will ensure you don't end up with a tangled mess in a drawer. Make sure there is plenty of clearance for any shelves within, and be mindful that some necklaces or bags might swing and bang when the door is opened and closed, so be selective about what hangs.

✓ If you only have a few formal handbags and you have enough hanging space, hang them with their outfits.

✓ Ties look beautiful rolled by hand and placed in a drawer lined with paper. It takes a little effort to maintain, but the reward is an attractive smorgasbord of ties.

Shoes

I confess that I am not a great fan of shoe racks, although they can be a good space maximiser. The problem with most racks is that they are not versatile enough and are not able to be stacked or added to easily – unless you are purchasing identical racks all at once. Simple, narrow shelving works well for shoes stored within a built-in cupboard.

You will need
- 30 minutes or more
- your shoes
- a rubbish bin
- an empty cardboard carton for taking excess shoes to the op shop

Method
1   Pair your shoes. Count the pairs.
2   Cull. Most of us wear about 20 per cent of our shoes 80 per cent of the time. Give your 20 per cent pole position at the front and centre of your storage space.
3   Shoe storage for children can be more organic: a row along the floor or the wardrobe, under the bed or 'free range' in a small, shallow basket. A deep container will create layers, making it difficult to find pairs.
4   Any shoes or boots that need repairing should be left near the front door to be taken to the cobbler as soon as possible.

Tips

✓ Box your best shoes and boots for maximum efficiency. You can purchase clear, stackable shoe and boot boxes that open from the end so that your shoes remain accessible, visible and dust-free (see ww.sorted.net.au/news/boxes.html).

✓ Laced shoes can be tied together and hung on hooks.

✓ If you have a shoe habit, invest in ample storage. Have a cabinet-maker customise your wardrobe storage to accommodate your collection.

✓ Old-fashioned hanging pockets aren't very stylish but work a treat on the inside of your wardrobe door.

✓ Shoe cupboards are unattractive! Cull shoes rather than invest in a specific item of furniture.

Clothes: hanging

If you do nothing else, invest in decent coathangers. Timber coathangers feel nice to use, look great and treat your clothes with respect. You'll save time on ironing as clothes won't be compressed and crease up again. Clothes won't be damaged by rusted metal, and flimsy plastic or wire hangers won't buckle under heavier items. Matching hangers look super-stylish too. Repetition is a powerful design technique.

You will need
- an hour or more
- all your hanging clothes (bring them all into the same room if necessary)
- strong, branded garbage bags (such as Glad) for taking excess clothes to the op shop – branded garbage bags are stronger than generic bags and are less likely to rip and tear

Method

1   Empty your wardrobe contents onto the floor or bed, sorting your clothes into categories as you go. How you go about this will depend on your lifestyle and the volume of any particular type of garment. Some ideas:

- *season*: hot, cold, mid-season
- *activity*: work, play, sleep, sport, formal
- *style*: T-shirts, trousers, frocks, jackets
- *colour blocking*: all reds, all oranges and so on (we can't do this in Melbourne because of the 'Melbourne black' phenomenon. I reckon over 80 per cent of what Melbournians wear is black)
- *size*: from long to short. Size is the best way to sort kids' clothes.

2   As you group your categories, decide what you *really* want or need (see 'Tips' below). Remove anything from the pile that needs laundering, mending or pressing. Put in your large plastic bag anything in good repair that can go to the op shop when you're done.

3   Rehang according to category. Ensure the longest items are hung at one end of your rail so that you can effectively use the space underneath the shorter items.

4   Make sure hangers – and the fronts of your garments – all face in the same direction for very efficient retrieval.

Tips

✓   Replace inferior hangers with good-quality ones as you rehang each item. (This includes decent skirt hangers too.)

✓   Fitted for Work is a fantastic recycling program. Donate your unwanted business clothing (in good repair), and Fitted for Work will distribute the clothing to disadvantaged women seeking to join or return to the workforce (see www.fittedforwork.org for information

on how to donate). Similar programs are run around the world –
I just wish there was a men's version somewhere!

✓ Don't ask yourself, 'Do I wear it?' It's too broad a question. Instead, ask yourself, 'When did I last wear it? How do I feel when I wear it? Is it comfortable? Do I love the colour? the fabric? the fit?'

✓ The clothes you need to keep are the clothes that hit the washing pile. The remainder will always be second best.

✓ Versatile pieces are best: think about what you'd ideally pack if you were travelling. Some examples are trousers that go with every-thing, a plain shirt that doesn't need ironing, your comfiest throw-on cardigan in a neutral colour, your favourite undies, the tie that matches the colour of your eyes, and the shoes that cost a fortune and that you have worn and worn.

✓ If you suspect you're missing a few crucial pieces, or if something needs replacing, make a list and plan to go shopping.

✓ Understand that some clothes look better on you than others. What necklines do you like? What cuts suit you best? What fabrics and colours do you favour? What do you love but know doesn't suit you (for me, it's orange and any cut that's not fitted on the bodice). Taking note of these things will save you from making expensive shopping errors. It will also make you a much more efficient shopper as you can go straight for the items you know you will love and wear. These days, noisy, scratchy clothing never even makes it into my wardrobe; I've learnt from my mistakes.

✓ Count the cost. If you paid $200 for a jacket and have worn it twice, it's worth $100 a wear. If you've worn it 200 times, its value is far greater as you've had a lot of good wear out of it. Give priority to the pieces that have earned their keep, and always keep an eye out for replacements as they won't last forever.

✓ Maintain your clothes. If a button needs sewing on, attend to it promptly – say, within a few weeks. Air and launder clothes when needed, including hand-washing.

✓ Are you a fan of the 'floordrobe'? That's fine, but make it part of your routine to clear the decks periodically and to hang, fold or wash what's there.

Clothes: drawers and shelves

The problem with most drawers is that they're too deep. If you have a drawer full of folded T-shirts stacked high, you are likely to wear only the top three or four. To get to those T-shirts at the bottom, you have to dig, which is too much like hard work. And it generally spoils all the effort you've made to carefully fold them in the first place. The other problem with deep drawers is that it's difficult to see what's what. Shallow drawers or, better still, shelves within a wardrobe are often a far more efficient way to store and see your clothes.

You will need
- an hour or more
- your folded clothes – bring them all into the same room if necessary
- strong, branded garbage bags (such as Glad) for taking excess clothes to the op shop

Method
1   Empty the contents of your drawers or shelves onto the floor or bed and sort your clothes however suits you best, bearing in mind the volume of any particular types of garments. For instance, you could sort by:
    - *season:* hot, cold, mid-season
    - *activity:* work, play, sleep, sport

- *style:* T-shirts, trousers
- *colour blocking:* all reds, all oranges, and so on. As you group your categories, decide what you *really* want or need (see 'Tips' below).

2 Refold if necessary. Learning to fold clothes like they do in shops (shop-folding) is easy, and it means that if your clothes crease, they crease in better places.

3 Ensure the fattest items, like jumpers, are placed in the lower and largest drawers or shelves.

4 Don't overcrowd your drawers: too many layers lead to inefficient retrieval.

Tips

✓ Deep drawers work best for jumpers and bulkier items.

✓ Shallow drawers are better for T-shirts and lightweight items.

✓ If you are short on drawers but have shelves, you can quickly and easily create 'drawers' by grabbing a sturdy cardboard carton (an archive box is best) and removing the lid.

✓ Heavy or cumbersome drawers should be banished. If they're sticky, then plane or sand them so they will slide easily. A little candle wax on the runners may also help. It will take just five minutes to grab a screwdriver and tighten any lose knobs. Better still, if the knobs or handles are a bit tired, update the look and replace them altogether.

✓ Line drawers with paper, nice card or wrapping paper to prevent timber snags or dust from messing with your clothes.

✓ Even better, use some old shoe boxes to segment your drawers for storing smaller items like socks and undies, bathers and stockings. Don't forget that children's shoe boxes can work just as well, if not better.

✓ Empty drawers completely from time to time. Items that have been pushed to the back or banished to the bottom might be of value. If it is 'dead wood', then get rid of it *now*.

●Out-of-season clothes

Out-of-season clothes are best packed into plastic bags when they are clean, mended and completely dry. Fold them neatly and pack them away. I am not a fan of those suction bags, as I have never had luck with them myself. Invariably, they pop back to normal when I least expect it. Any kind of plastic bag is OK, but clear ones will give you visual clarity. Label them regardless of the type of bag you use. Pack the bags away up high at the top of a wardrobe or, if you must, under the bed.

A cardboard carton offers greater versatility when it comes time to store out-of-season clothes as boxes stack and plastic bags don't. Clear plastic tubs are OK too, *provided* you only have a few.

You can also store out-of-season clothes in your empty suitcases. For ease of use, bag the clothes first. That way, if you need to remove them to use your case, they remain contained and manageable.

Glossary

chaosification   Television's 'Super Nanny', Jo Frost, once surveyed a frantic home and exclaimed, 'Look at all this chaosification!' I think she meant 'What a complete disaster!'

critter   This is what I call anything small. It is often also something useful.

decision fatigue   An inability to make decisions, which tends to strike when too many decisions need to be made.

double-buying   When you purchase something you already own because you have 'lost' the original.

efficiency   Productivity with minimum wasted effort or expense.

ephemera   Any item that is designed to exist for a short period of time; for example, brochures, tickets, timetables.

faff   To faff is to waste time or energy.

floordrobe   This refers to the practice of using the floor to store clothes that would normally be hung up in a wardrobe.

inertia   Inertia is inactivity, lack of energy, a sluggish or static state.

litmus test   Technically this is a scientific test to read the PH levels for acidity, it is also a colloquial term to indicate the bottom line: good or bad, positive or negative.

manky I use it to mean old and crusty, dirty, or not in good repair.

minutiae This is the fine detail, the little things.

mixed bag This is the term I use for anything unsorted, usually mixed types (for instance, paper, clothing and stationery in the same area or storage receptacle).

plug into This is the act of adding to an empty existing space or system.

productivity This indicates a state of producing much (in terms or quality and/or quantity).

schmick This is a way to describe something that is particularly special and lovely, or attractive in appearance.

stuff This term covers all the physical objects that populate our lives, including personal items, clobber, furniture, goods and chattels, appliances, ornaments, belongings, memorabilia, things, tools, flotsam and jetsam, material possessions, clothing, home wares, paperwork, junk and equipment.

visual clutter This is when you look at something and all you can see is a mess.

white space This term refers to an unencumbered space where the eye can rest. The creation of white space is a popular design technique in print, particularly in magazines and in digital design (such as website design).

Websites

There are so many great ways to recycle your unwanted goods; here are my top six resources:

- **www.fittedforwork.org**
  If you have unwanted business clothing that is still in good condition, why not donate it to the Fitted for Work program, which provides business clothes for disadvantaged women who want to return to work. It's a fantastic example of 'old' being turned into 'new' and is the perfect recycling resource for anyone with a social conscience.

- **www.freecycle.org/groups/australia**
  Freecycle is a form of recycling (or giving) that hooks up unwanted goods with new owners. Children's toys, a kitchen sink, old computers or even a box of earthworms are just some of the free items that have been on offer around the world.

- **www.unicef.org.au**
  Foreign currency (or Australian currency for that matter) can be donated to UNICEF's Change for Good program. If you're flying Qantas soon, use the envelope supplied on board, or check out UNICEF's website for other locations where you can donate.

- **www.mobilephonerecyling.com.au**
  By donating your unwanted mobile phone, you'll prevent highly toxic materials ending up in landfill. Every phone collected will also help raise funds for a charity or organisation in your state.

- **www.rspca.org.au/localsites**

  Old towels and blankets are welcome at the RSPCA around Australia. There are a variety of drop-off points, so get in touch to find out where the closest one to you is.

- **www.recyclingnearyou.com.au**

  This is where you can go to find out everything you've ever wanted to know about recycling in your area but were afraid to ask. I love this site – it's so comprehensive!

For a more comprehensive list of web resources with a recycling slant, visit www.sorted.net.au/links.

Contact details

I love feedback. If there is anything in this book you'd like to comment on, please let me know. What was most useful? What most inspired you? Or what would you like to see in a revised edition? Please write to me at sorted@sorted.net.au.

Consultations

I am available:

- for one-to-one sessions in your home or workplace
- to create and run workshops and training sessions
- to write material for your newsletters, intranet or publication.

Please contact me at info@sorted.net.au.

Further reading

You might like to check out these great books on the following topics:

Clutter

Nelson, Mike, *Stop Clutter from Stealing Your Life*, New Page Books, Franklin Lakes, NJ, 2001.

Passoff, Michele, *Lighten Up! Free Yourself from Clutter*, HarperPerennial, New York, 1998.

Efficiency

Covey, Stephen R, *7 Habits of Highly Effective People*, Simon & Schuster, New York, 2003.

Procrastination

Tracy, Brian, *Eat That Frog! 21 Great Ways to Stop Procrastinating and Get More Done in Less Time*, Berrett-Koehler Publishers, San Francisco, 2007.

Passing on unwanted items

Duncan, Dianne, *Let's Haggle: the Fun Guide to Garage Sales, Op Shops and Markets*, Dunell Books, Traralgon, Victoria, 2003.

www.sorted.net.au/links

Emotional wellbeing

Carlson, Richard, *Don't Sweat the Small Stuff – and It's All Small Stuff*, Hyperion, New York, 1997.

Hay, Louise L, *You Can Heal Your Life*, Hay House, Santa Monica, CA, 1987.

Schaef, Anne Wilson, *Meditations for Women Who Do Too Much*, HarperCollins, San Francisco, 2004.

Acknowledgements

Working as a hands-on Professional Organiser over the years has been a thoroughly rewarding role and one that would not have been possible without the generosity of my clients, who have allowed me into their homes, workplaces and lives. Together we've created some sensational results and I thank you for that joyous opportunity. Confidentiality means I cannot name names, but here's a big shout out to you all! Thanks also to all involved in the production of this book.

Finally, thanks to my dad, Gavin Oliver, for allowing me to be me.

Credits

The author and publishers would like to gratefully credit or acknowledge the following for permission to reproduce copyright material:
Bob Geldof for quote on p. 3; The Andy Warhol Museum for extract on p. 3 from www.warhol.org/collections/archives.html, © 2006 The Andy Warhol Museum, a museum of Carnegie Institute; Frank Lloyd Wright for quote on p. 6. Frank Lloyd Wright quote is used with permission of The Frank Lloyd Wright Foundation, Taliesin West, Scotsdale, AZ.; Deirdre Macken for extract on p. 10 from 'Get Organised Month: the Stuff of Nightmares for Hoarders', *Australian Financial Review*, 20 January 2007; *New Scientist* for quote on p. 37 from edition dated 28 May 2005, page 28; James Arthur Ray for quote on p. 37.

Index

About the author

Lissanne Oliver is Australia's most well-known and experienced Professional Organiser.

A veteran of the organising industry, Lissanne is a founding member of the Australasian Association of Professional Organisers. She's been instrumental in raising the profile of the profession and dramatically increasing its growth.

You may also recognise Lissanne from her television work as a presenter on *Your Life on the Lawn* and *Better Homes & Gardens*. Her extensive repertoire of ideas, tips and expertise is frequently featured in major metropolitan dailies and your favourite lifestyle and business publications. Lissanne is a regular guest on ABC radio and writes a hugely popular newsletter and blog.

Lissanne's true expertise lies in assisting people to better organise their space, work, life or home. Lissanne combines organising with creativity to problem-solve a wide range of organisational and efficiency issues.

Considered a national authority on all things organising, she's a qualified trainer who runs a business called SORTED! (www.sorted.net.au) that offers a range of practical services and clever products.